AUSTRALIA

THE LITTLE
AUSSIE COOKBOOK

CREDITS

Published by – Honeysett Publications Pty Ltd (Inc NSW)
PO Box 23, Westgate NSW 2048 Australia

Edited by – George Jaksic & Michelle Miran
Designed by – George Jaksic
Cartoons by – Noel Slapp

Typeset in Antique Olive by Honeysett Typesetters Pty Ltd (Inc NSW)
Printed by – Honeysett Instant Print Pty Ltd (Inc NSW)
40 Norton Street, Leichhardt NSW 2040 Australia   Tel (02) 569 8133
© Copyright G. Jaksic, M. Miran 1984

National Library of Australia card number and ISBN 0 9592229 1 X

Fourth impression April 1985

FOREWORD

In the early days of European settlement in Australia, food was scarce and many months would go by before supplies would arrive from Great Britain. If only the colony's first settlers had taken survival lessons from the Aborigines they would have had a wonderfully wholesome diet! Instead, they tried to cultivate types of crops which were unsuitable to local conditions and took a long time to grow.

Consequently, those first years were filled with extreme hardship. It is not surprising that pioneering women who had to work with limited resources in harsh conditions to feed their families created foods such as damper and parrot pie. The Aborigines, on the other hand, were skilled hunters and gatherers who could provide a nutritious meal from their natural environment:– yabbies and barramundi from rivers and streams, goanna and kangaroo meat cooked in underground ovens, insects and wild fruit from the bush.

Over the last 200 years Australia has developed a distinctive cuisine bringing together the flavours and styles of a multiplicity of cultures.Indeed where else would you be able to select from a choice of peking duck, falafel, tacos, croissants or paella? In whatever Australian city you travel you will find a casual outdoors lifestyle which is made possible by long hot summers and mild winters. Wherever you are either strolling along Bondi Beach, Sydney or through Rundle Mall, Adelaide you can savour luscious tidbits such as satays, gelati or the famous Aussie meat pie.

The year round availability and the extensive variety of fruit, vegetables, seafood and meat enables a diversity in entertaining styles from lavish haute cuisine to the traditional Sunday barbie.

All Australians, whatever their origins, whether they come from convict settlers, the orient or the mediterranean, show a common desire to be outside enjoying life, either at the football, at the beach or wandering through a natural reserve. Friends and families gather together to enjoy anything from a barbecue prawn to bratwurst with a cold beer or a dry red.

Australian cuisine is unique because it has drawn from all corners of the globe bringing together traditions, tastes and ideas to form a melting pot which reflects the colour and characteristics of this vast land down under.

With our Bicentennial year of 1988 not long away, there is a growing excitement on a national scale – about *our* Australia.

We hope that through the recipes in THE LITTLE AUSSIE COOKBOOK you are able to share in the delights of traditional Australian fare.

Michelle Miran & George Jaksic

OTHER PUBLICATIONS

Edited by
George Jaksic & Michelle Miran, 1983

Distributed by
Desco Pacific Wholesale
GPO Box 160, Suva, Fiji Islands
Telephone 31 3477, Telex 2319 NLDC FJ
Cables "Desai" Suva

EDITORS' NOTES

THE LITTLE AUSSIE COOKBOOK incorporates traditional Australian fare and a variety of recipes from our multicultural heritage. It should be noted that recipes vary in content and method, according to local influences, but the overall style has been kept as uniform as possible. Ingredients may be added, omitted, varied in nature or quantity in cooking, to suit your own tastes and preferences.

If you have any comments about recipes, or suggestions for future editions, we would be pleased to hear from you – please direct all correspondence to the publishers.

The recipes in THE LITTLE AUSSIE COOKBOOK have been gathered from a variety of institutions – and also individuals who have chosen to share their family favourites.

We wish to thank all the contributors who have cooperated and assisted us with this collection of recipes.

Special thanks to James Carpenter, Michele Bugden, Andrew Page, Dominic Lattari, Virginia Walker, Leslie Bucknell and all of the production crew.

M.M. & G.J.

IMPORTANT NOTE

Measures in THE LITTLE AUSSIE COOKBOOK comply with the Standards Association of Australia. They are based on **level** measures. Quantities have been expressed in round figures, in metric and imperial measures.

TABLE OF CONTENTS

WEIGHTS
& MEASURES

TERMS

g	= gram	mm	= millimetre
kg	= kilogram	cm	= centimetre
ml	= millilitre	°C	= degrees Celcius
l	= litre	°F	= degrees Fahrenheit

SOLID MEASURES

15g = ½ ounce
30g = 1 ounce (approx. weight 30g)
125g = 4 ounces (approx. weight 125g)
250g = 8 ounces (approx. weight 250g)
375g = 12 ounces (approx. weight 375g)
500g = 1 pound (approx. weight 500g)
1kg = 2 pounds (approx. weight 1000g)

LIQUID MEASURES

5ml = 1 teaspoon
20ml = 1 tablespoon
30ml = 1 fluid ounce
125ml = 4 fluid ounces or ½ cup
250ml = 8 fluid ounces or 1 cup

LENGTH MEASURES

2mm = 1/16 inch
3mm = ⅛ inch
5mm = ¼ inch
1cm = ½ inch
2cm = ¾ inch
2.5cm = 1 inch
4cm = 1½ inches
5cm = 2 inches

OVEN TEMPERATURES

Keep Warm	80°C = 175°F
Cool	100°C = 200°F
Very Slow	120°C = 250°F
Slow	150°C = 300°F
Moderately Slow	160°C = 325°F
Moderate	180°C = 350°F
Moderately Hot	190°C = 375°F
Hot	200°C = 400°F
Very Hot	230°C = 450°F

APPETISERS
& ENTREES

KOSCIUSKO SMOKED TROUT PATE

1 whole smoked trout, 300g (10oz)
1 cup water
½ cup dry white wine
125g (¼lb) butter
2 teaspoons gelatine
300ml (10 fl oz) sour cream
salt
pepper
1 small ripe avocado
lemon juice

Carefully remove skin and bones from trout. Place skin and head of trout into pan, add water and wine. Bring to boil, reduce heat, simmer covered for 5 minutes. Strain through fine sieve. Return liquid to pan, add butter and gelatine, stir over low heat until butter has melted and gelatine dissolved. Place liquid into blender, add trout meat. Blend on medium speed for 3 minutes or until finely pureed. Pour into bowl, leave until cold. Fold in sour cream, season with salt and pepper. Pour into 4 individual serving dishes. Cover and refrigerate overnight. Just before serving, remove skin and seed from avocado, cut into thin slices, toss lightly in lemon juice, arrange on top of trout pate. *Serves 4.*

CHICKEN LIVER PATE

250g (½lb) chicken livers
1 small onion
⅓ cup chicken stock
¼ teaspoon curry powder
½ teaspoon salt
pinch pepper
2 teaspoons worcestershire sauce
100g (3oz) butter

Simmer chicken livers and onion in chicken stock for about 5 minutes. Add next 5 ingredients to cooked chicken livers and allow to cool. Put cooled ingredients into blender and whirl until smooth. Add the butter gradually, whirling blender after each addition. Pour pate into serving dish and chill. *Serves 4-6.*

SMOKED OYSTER DIP

180g (6oz) cream cheese
1 tablespoon cream or top milk
1 teaspoon seasoned salt
2 teaspoons worcestershire sauce
1 x 100g (3oz) can smoked oysters
2 teaspoons grated onion
1 teaspoon finely chopped chives
salt and pepper

▶

Soften cream cheese and beat in cream or milk until smooth. Add seasoned salt and sauce. Cut oysters into small pieces and mix into cheese with onion. Thin with cream or milk if desired. Sprinkle with chives. *Serves 4-6.*

GRILLED BANANA PRAWNS

10 green banana prawns, with shells
2 tablespoons olive oil
2 cloves garlic, crushed
½ teaspoon salt

Place the prawns intact with their shells in a baking dish. Brush with oil and sprinkle with garlic and salt. Grill the prawns about 10cm (4in) from a preheated griller for 3-4 minutes on each side. *Serves 4.*

NED KELLY'S EYE

2 slices thick white bread
2 eggs
2 tablespoons butter
2 tablespoons oil

Using a 2½ cm (1in) biscuit cutter remove the centre of the bread. Melt the butter, add the oil and heat. Place the bread in the hot fat. Break the egg into the centre and fry until the egg white is almost set. Turn to brown. The remaining pieces of bread from the centre should be fried until crisp. Serve with grilled bacon and tomato for breakfast. *Serves 2.*

SEAFOOD CREPES

pancake batter for 6 to 8 pancakes
250g (½lb) peeled prawns (shrimps)
120g (¼lb) can drained crabmeat
1 x 450g (1lb) can cream of celery soup
125g (¼lb) mushrooms,
sliced and lightly cooked in
2 tablespoons butter
2 tablespoons sour cream
2 tablespoons white wine

Make pancakes, keep warm. Combine prawns, crab, ⅓ cup celery soup, and half of the cooked mushrooms in a saucepan. Bring to boil, then simmer 3 minutes. Combine remaining soup, mushrooms, cream and wine. Simmer 3 minutes. Divide seafood filling between pancakes and roll up. Place in serving dish. Spoon sauce over. *Serves 4-6.*

SCOTCH EGGS

12 hard-boiled eggs, shelled
750g (1½lb) sausage meat
1 tablespoon mixed herbs
1 tablespoon parsley
salt and pepper
seasoned flour (salt, pepper and mustard)
1 beaten egg
breadcrumbs

Mix the sausage meat with herbs, parsley, salt and pepper, and pat out into circles. Place 1 egg on each piece of meat and fold around. Roll in seasoned flour, add beaten egg and then breadcrumbs. Fry well, cool and cut into halves. *Serves 6-8.*

ZUCCHINI BLOSSOM FRITTERS

20 zucchini blossoms
2 cups flour
1 cup milk
4 eggs, beaten
olive oil
salt

Remove the blossoms from the squash. Open the blossoms and remove the pistils. Wash the blossoms gently to avoid damaging them and lay them on a linen cloth to dry. Prepare the batter by mixing the flour to a smooth paste with the milk. Add the paste to the eggs and mix. For a crisp frying batter, do not add salt at this point. Gently take one blossom at a time and dip it in the batter. Let any excess batter drip off and put the blossom into a pot of oil heated to 180°C (350°F) frying only a few at a time. Turn the fritters until they are golden brown and crisp on all sides. Remove with a slotted spoon and drain on absorbent paper. Sprinkle with salt while they are still hot. Arrange the crisp fritters on a serving dish and serve immediately. Serves 6-8.

RABBIT PATE

1 large rabbit
150ml (5 fl oz) dry white wine
500g (1lb) lean veal
60g (2oz) streaky bacon plus
extra for lining the dish
250g (½lb) chicken livers
¼ teaspoon marjoram
2 cloves crushed garlic
salt and pepper
1 egg

▶

Trim all the flesh from the ribs of the rabbit and the giblets, liver, lights and heart, chop finely. Place in a bowl and cover with the wine. Trim the remaining flesh off the bone and mince with the veal, chicken liver and bacon. Add to the marinated meats with the herbs and the egg. Line an earthenware dish with the remaining bacon. Pour in the meat mixture and cover with foil. Cook for 1¼-1½ hours at 180°C (350°F). Remove from the oven and place a heavy plate on top to weigh down. Cool and serve with wholemeal bread. *Serves 6.*

ANGELS ON HORSEBACK

**12 fresh oysters
6 thin slices bacon
3 slices hot buttered toast
each cut into squares
parsley sprigs**

Simmer the oysters in their own liquor over low heat for 4-5 minutes. Drain and wrap each oyster in a half slice of bacon. Secure bacon with toothpicks. Place under a hot griller until bacon is crisp. Serve on squares of hot buttered toast. Garnish with parsley. *Serves 4.*

DEVILS ON HORSEBACK

**12 large dried cooking prunes
½ cup red wine
1 bay leaf**

Stuffing
**12 anchovy fillets,
curled round 12 almonds**

Or
12 teaspoons chutney

Or
**12 pimento stuffed olives
6 thin slices bacon
parsley sprigs**

Place prunes or plums in a saucepan. Add wine and bay leaf. Simmer over low heat for 20 minutes until just tender. Cool prunes in the wine and remove pips. Fill each prune with one of the stuffings. Wrap ½ a bacon slice round each prune and secure with a toothpick. Place in a small baking dish. Heat in a 200°C (400°F) oven for 10-12 minutes until bacon is crisp. Drain on paper towels. Place on a serving dish and garnish with parsley. *Serves 4.*

SOUPS

BEER SOUP

2 cups milk
1 stick cinnamon
1 piece lemon peel, 3cm (1in) wide
1 tablespoon sugar
2 tablespoons cornflour
¼ cup cold water
1 370ml (12 fl oz) can beer
1 egg yolk, slightly beaten
parsley

In a saucepan, combine milk, cinnamon, lemon peel and sugar, bring to boil. Reduce heat, simmer 10 minutes. Dissolve cornflour in cold water, stir into milk mixture. Continue to cook, stirring constantly, until thickened. Stir in beer, heat. Beat a small amount of hot beer mixture into egg, return to saucepan. Stir well. Remove from heat, strain. Serve hot or cold. Garnish with parsley. *Serves 4-6.*

TASMANIAN SCALLOP SOUP

60g (2oz) butter
250g (½lb) carrots, diced
3 onions, chopped
500g (1lb) scallops, sliced
¼ teaspoon thyme
½ bay leaf
3 tablespoons chopped parsley
salt and pepper
250ml (8 fl oz) white wine
1½ litres (2pt) fish stock
750g (1½lb) potatoes
250ml (8 fl oz) cream
pinch cayenne

Melt the butter, add the carrots and onions, simmer for 10 minutes. Add the scallops, herbs, salt and pepper, wine and stock, simmer 10 minutes. Add the potatoes and cook until tender. Puree in a food processor, add the cream and heat gently, sprinkle with cayenne and serve with warm damper. Serves 4-6.

EGG AND LEMON SOUP

8 cups clear chicken stock
½ to ¾ cup rice, vermicelli or small pasta
3 eggs
lemons, juice
½ teaspoon salt
black pepper, freshly ground

Bring chicken broth to the boil. Add the rice or vermicelli and simmer for 15 minutes. Meanwhile, beat the eggs until frothy. Slowly add the lemon juice to the eggs, beating constantly. Add 1½ to 2 cups of the broth, 1 tablespoon at a time, beating constantly. Remove the remaining broth from the heat and beat in the egg mixture. Season with salt and pepper and serve immediately. Serves 4-6.

FENNEL SOUP

2 large cleaned fennel bulbs, sliced
2 medium potatoes, diced
1 leek or onion, chopped
2 tablespoons butter
6 cups chicken stock
salt and pepper
1 cup cream
¼ cup chopped mint

In a heavy saucepan melt the butter and saute the fennel, potatoes and onion, cook for 5 minutes. Pour the stock onto the vegetables, cover and simmer for 30 minutes. Puree in a food processor, return to the pan and season with salt and pepper. Add the cream and heat gently, serve garnished with chopped mint. *Serves 4-6*.

OXTAIL SOUP

1 oxtail
1 onion, chopped
2 carrots, diced
1 turnip, diced
1 parsnip, diced
3 sticks celery, chopped
1 tablespoon butter
3-4 juniper berries
salt and pepper
2½ litres (4pts) beef stock

Chop the oxtail into pieces, cover with cold water and soak overnight. Melt the butter and brown the oxtail. Add the vegetables and cook for 2-3 minutes. Add the herbs, salt and pepper, juniper berries and stock. Bring to the boil and simmer for 3-4 hours. Adjust the seasonings and serve with hot damper or crusty bread. *Serves 4-6*.

YELLOW SPLIT PEA SOUP

1 cup yellow split peas
2 onions, chopped
3 carrots, diced
2 sticks celery, chopped

▶

500g (1lb) smoked pork, diced
salt and pepper
2½ litres (4pts) chicken stock

Place the peas in a bowl with cold water, cover and stand overnight. Next day, drain and place the peas in a deep saucepan with the remaining ingredients. Cover with the stock, simmer for 2½-3 hours or until the peas are cooked. Serve with fried croutons. *Serves 4-6.*

VEGETABLE SOUP

½ cabbage, shredded
4 carrots, diced
2 leeks, washed and sliced
½ bunch spinach, shredded
2 parsnips, diced
1 turnip, diced
3-4 sticks celery, chopped
3 medium potatoes, diced
1 tin peeled tomatoes
250g (½lb) gravy beef, diced
250g (½lb) smoked pork, diced
salt and pepper
2½ litres (4pts) rich beef stock

Place the meats in a deep saucepan and allow to brown in their own fat. Add all the vegetables, cook for 3-4 minutes. Cover with the stock, salt and pepper. Cover and simmer for 3-4 hours. Serve with grated parmesan cheese on top. *Serves 4-6.*

CREAM OF CARROT SOUP

500g (1lb) carrots
1 litre (2pt) chicken stock
(or water and stock cubes)
chopped parsley
250g (½lb) tomatoes
350ml (12 fl oz) milk
90g (3oz) butter
salt and pepper

Slice carrots, peel and chop tomatoes. Melt butter in a heavy pan and cook the carrots gently for 3 minutes stirring now and then. Add tomatoes and cook a further 2 minutes. Pour in heated stock and season with salt and pepper. Simmer until carrots are soft. Put through a mouli sieve or blender. Return to cleaned pan, add hot milk, and season. Serve sprinkled with chopped chives. *Serves 4-6.*

CHEESE SOUP

60g (2oz) butter
2 tablespoons flour
3 cups chicken stock
1 cup milk
salt and pepper
nutmeg
2 egg yolks
1 cup cream
1 cup grated tasty cheese

Garnish
croutons
chopped leek

Melt butter, stir in flour cook for 1 minute, stir in stock and milk, bring to boil and add seasonings. Beat egg yolks with the cream and stir into soup. Do not boil. Stir in cheese until it melts. Serve with croutons and chopped leeks. *Serves 4-6.*

BUTTERNUT PUMPKIN SOUP

6 small butternut pumpkins
2 onions
60g (2oz) butter

2 cups chicken stock
salt and pepper
nutmeg
1 bayleaf
150ml (4 fl oz) cream
2 tablespoons grated gruyere cheese

Cut the tops off the pumpkins, scrape seeds from bottom half of shells, sprinkle with salt and put a ball of aluminium foil in each. Scrape flesh from pumpkin tops and reserve for soup. Bake pumpkin shells and tops in 180°C (350°F) oven for 30 minutes. Chop onions and saute in butter until soft. Add chopped pumpkin, chicken stock, salt and pepper, nutmeg and bayleaf, and simmer for approximately 25 minutes, or until soft. Blend all ingredients, or put them through a sieve. Keep soup warm. Just before serving, add cream and gruyere cheese. Serve in pumpkin shells with lids on top. *Serves 4-6.*

CHICKEN & VERMICELLI SOUP

2 chicken breasts
1½ litres (2pt) chicken stock
2 tablespoons fish sauce, to taste
5 dried mushrooms
1 packet white vermicelli
3 shallots

▶

Cook chicken breasts in the stock with fish sauce until cooked. Try to keep the stock as clear as possible. Take the chicken out and shred into long thin strips. Put them aside. Soak dried mushrooms in hot water for approximately 10 minutes to soften them, then cut off their stems. Rinse them well in cold water and cut them into small strips. Soak vermicelli in warm water and cut into pieces to facilitate serving. Put mushrooms and the white part of shallots into the chicken stock and boil for 5 minutes, then add vermicelli. When vermicelli becomes transparent, add chicken. Finally chop green part of shallots into small pieces and mix them well. The soup is served with pepper. *Serves 4-6.*

BEAN SOUP

500g (1lb) dried haricot beans
10 cups water
1 smoked pork hock
3 medium onions, chopped
1 carrot, finely chopped
1½ tablespoons chopped parsley
2 tablespoons chopped celery leaves
2 tablespoons tomato puree
1½ tablespoons olive oil
½ teaspoon salt
freshly ground black pepper

Soak the beans overnight. Wash, drain and place them in a large saucepan. Add the water and boil for 2 minutes. Pour off all the water and add the same quantity of fresh water. Bring to boil, add the pork, onions, carrot, 1 tablespoon parsley, celery leaves, tomato puree, oil, salt and pepper. Simmer for about 2 hours or until the beans and pork are soft and tender. Season, sprinkle on the remaining parsley and serve hot. *Serves 4-6.*

CAPRICORNIA CRAB SOUP

500g (1lb) crab shells
1 teaspoon salt
1 green chilli, chopped
2 tomatoes, diced
4 cups water
1 small onion, diced
1 small carrot, diced
100g (3oz) crab meat, raw
1 small lime

Place the first 6 ingredients in a heavy saucepan and simmer for 30 minutes. Strain. Add the diced carrot and crab meat. Simmer 7-10 minutes. Season and garnish with chopped coriander and lime slices. *Serves 4.*

SEAFOOD

PORT JACKSON FISH PARCELS

6 fish cutlets (schnapper)
salt and pepper
lemon juice
2 tablespoons fresh chopped dill
60g (2oz) butter

Place each piece of fish on a sheet of foil. Sprinkle with salt and pepper, dill, lemon juice and dots of butter. Wrap firmly and bake or barbeque for 20-25 minutes. Open and serve with lemon slices. *Serves 6.*

SEAFOOD KEBABS

Marinade
¼ cup olive oil
2 cloves garlic
¼ cup chopped parsley
¼ cup lemon juice
½ teaspoon oregano
salt and pepper

250g (½lb) banana prawns, shelled
250g (½lb) Tasmanian scallops
cherry tomatoes
pickling onions, peeled
bamboo skewers

Combine all the ingredients for the marinade, add the prawns and scallops. Refrigerate for 1-2 hours. Thread the prawns, scallops, onions and tomatoes alternately onto the skewers. Grill or barbeque for 10 minutes, brushing with the remaining marinade occasionally. Serve on a bed of hot buttered rice. *Serves 4.*

SNOWY MOUNTAINS RAINBOW TROUT ALMONDINE

4 x 250g (½lb) whole trout cleaned
1 cup milk
½ cup flour seasoned with ½ teaspoon salt
freshly ground black pepper
250g (½lb) butter
⅓ cup sliced almonds
parsley for garnish
lemon wedges

Dry trout with paper towels. Dip in milk and then in flour. Heat ¾ of the butter in a large skillet. Fry trout five minutes on each side over moderate heat until golden brown. Sprinkle fish with salt and pepper and keep hot. In a small skillet, heat remaining butter and lightly brown the almonds. Place trout on a hot platter. Pour the butter and almonds over the trout. Garnish with parsley and lemon wedges. *Serves 4.*

NICK'S FISH AND CHIPS

750g (1½lb) fish fillets, eg. gemfish, cod, flounder
1 tablespoon lemon juice
½ cup flour

Beer Batter
1 cup flour
1 teaspoon salt
freshly ground black pepper
1 teaspoon paprika
1 cup beer

Chips
3 large potatoes
1 teaspoon salt
oil for deep frying

Cut the fish into medium sized pieces allowing 2 pieces for each serving, and sprinkle the fish with lemon juice. Combine the ingredients for the batter in a bowl stirring with a whisk until smooth. Peel the potatoes, cut into slices and then into chips. Place the chips in a bowl of iced water for 10 minutes. Drain potatoes and dry them on paper towels. Heat the fat to 190°C (375°F). Fry the potatoes until they are almost tender, but not browned. Drain chips on paper towels. Dredge the fish in flour and then dip in the batter. Fry the fish for 5 minutes in the same oil in which chips have been cooked and remove the fish from the fat. Increase the heat under the fat until it regains a temperature of 190°C (375°F). Lower the fish into the hot fat and continue cooking for 3 or 4 minutes until batter is crisp and golden. Drain the fish and keep it warm in a 150°C (300°F) oven. Return the chips to the oil and fry for 3 or 4 minutes until tender, crisp and golden. Drain the chips and sprinkle with coarse salt. Serve the fish and chips immediately, preferably in an old newspaper wrapper. *Serves 4.*

WHITING WITH MANDARIN SEGMENTS

8 whiting fillets
1 x 450g (1lb) can vegetable soup
1½ tablespoons vinegar
1½ tablespoons brown sugar
1 tablespoon cornflour blended
with a little water
1 300g (10oz) can mandarins, drained

Skin and bone fish fillets, roll up and secure with a toothpick. Place in a shallow oven proof dish. Combine remaining ingredients in small saucepan and bring to the boil, stirring frequently. Pour sauce over fish. Cover and bake at 180°C (350°F) for 20 minutes. *Serves 4.*

LONGREEF TUNA STEAKS

4 fresh tuna steaks

Marinade
½ **cup olive oil**
2-3 cloves crushed garlic
½ **cup chopped parsley**
juice of 1 lemon
½ **teaspoon freshly ground black pepper**
salt

This dish is best prepared on a barbecue. Combine all the ingredients for the marinade, place in a shallow dish and lay the tuna fish in it. Allow to marinade for 3-4 hours turning occasionally. Cook on a hot barbecue or grill, and baste with the marinade. The fish will take 10-12 minutes to cook. *Serves 4.*

GRANDMA MACCONACHIE'S BAKED HADDOCK

500g (1lb) cooked flaked smoked haddock or cod
2 eggs
½ **cup cream**
½ **teaspoon salt**
¼ **teaspoon pepper**

½ **teaspoon paprika**
1 tablespoon lemon juice
2 tablespoons melted butter
1 tablespoon chives, chopped
½ **chopped green capsicum**
½ **stick chopped celery**

Combine ingredients thoroughly. Place in a greased casserole dish, bake in moderate oven 200°C (400°F) for 25 minutes. *Serves 4.*

BAKED AVOCADO SEAFOOD

2 avocadoes
¼ **cup lemon juice**
250g (¼lb) shelled, cooked prawns
250g (¼lb) Sydney rock oysters
1 cup white sauce
½ **cup parmesan cheese**
1 teaspoon paprika

Slice the avocadoes and sprinkle with the lemon juice. Mix the seafood into the white sauce with half the cheese. Fill the avocado cavity with the mixture, top with cheese and sprinkle with the paprika. Bake at 190°C (375°F) for 10 minutes. Serve garnished with lemon. *Serves 4.*

TROPICAL SEAFOOD SALAD

1 large paw paw (papaya)
2 ripe avocadoes
¼ cup lime juice
1½kg (3½lb) cooked mixed seafood –
prawns, scallops, mussels, calamari
and baby octopus
¼ cup French dressing
freshly ground black pepper

Peel the paw paw, cut lengthwise into strips, then arrange on a flat platter. Peel and slice the avocado and pour the lime juice over to prevent browning. Mix together the seafood, French dressing and black pepper. Pile onto the paw paw. Top with the avocado. Chill and serve as an entree or main course. *Serves 4.*

Batter
1½ cups flour
1 teaspoon curry powder
½ teaspoon salt
1 egg
½ cup soda water
½ cup chopped macadamia nuts

Wash and pat dry the seafood. Sift the flour, curry powder and salt into a bowl. Separate the egg and mix the yolk with the soda water, then stir into the flour to make a smooth batter. Stir in the chopped nuts. Beat the egg white until stiff and fold into the batter. Dip the seafood into the batter and deep fry 3-4 pieces at a time, drain and serve a combination in individual dishes. *Serves 6.*

MACADAMIA SEAFOOD BASKET

250g (½lb) Tasmanian scallops
250g (½lb) royal red prawns
250g (½lb) squid rings
250g (½lb) lobster or Balmain bug meat
4 gemfish fillets
oil for deep frying

GOLD COAST PRAWN BOAT

1kg (2lb) large King Prawns, cooked
1 pineapple
½ lettuce
glace cherries
cocktail sauce
toothpicks

▶

Cut pineapple lengthways into six pieces, leaving green top intact. Cut fruit away from skin and slice into pieces. Replace on pineapple skin, decorate, and fix with toothpicks and cherries. Lay pineapple on bed of lettuce on an oval silver or crockery plate, and place prawns on top of pineapple. Mayonnaise sauce may be served as an accompaniment. *Serves 4.*

YOU BEAUT BARBECUE PRAWNS
(HOGE'S BARBECUE SHRIMPS)

**1kg (2½lb) green banana prawns
(or tiger prawns)**

Marinade
**½ cup Australian whisky
3-4 cloves garlic, crushed
1 teaspoon grated ginger
grated rind of 1 orange
½ cup orange juice
125g (4oz) melted butter
salt and pepper**

Wash the prawns (or shrimp) and leave the shells intact. Combine all the ingredients and marinade for 2-3 hours. Barbecue for 6-8 minutes, brushing liberally with the marinade while cooking. *Serves 4.*

MR LEE'S CURRIED PRAWNS

**750g (1½lb) prawns
2 tablespoons butter
1 onion, finely sliced
1 apple, grated
1 banana, sliced
3 tablespoons flour
1 tablespoon curry powder
1½ teaspoons ginger powder
2 tablespoons soy sauce
1¾ cups stock
3 tablespoons Chinese sweet pickle**

Shell prawns. Melt butter, fry onion until golden brown. Add apple and banana and fry lightly. Add flour, curry powder and ginger, cook for about 2 minutes. Mix in soy sauce and stock. Stir until mixture boils and thickens. Add pickle, prawns and simmer for 10 minutes. Serve with boiled rice and side dishes of coconut, chutney, sultanas, etc. Garnish with lemon and toasted coconut. *Serves 4.*

BRANDIED BALMAIN BUGS

**4 green bugs per person
¼ cup olive oil**

2 cloves garlic
¼ cup chopped spring onion
2 tablespoons chopped celery tops
½ cup brandy
1 cup dry white wine
1 tablespoon tomato paste
½ teaspoon fresh thyme
pinch pepper
¼ teaspoon paprika
2 tablespoons parsley
2 tablespoons cream
salt

Wash the bugs and cut lengthways. Heat the olive oil in a large frying pan. Add the garlic and the bugs, cook over a high heat until the bugs start to turn red. Add the spring onion and celery, flame with brandy. When the flame dies down pour in the wine and add the tomato paste, thyme, pepper, paprika, parsley, cream and salt. Cover and cook over a low heat for 3 minutes and serve immediately. *Serves 4.*

BALMAIN BUG BOUILLABAISSE

500g (1lb) Balmain bug meat
20 mussels
1 medium rock lobster

200g (6oz) squid
200g (6oz) scallops
2 cloves crushed garlic
2 cups white wine
bouquet garni
4 cups water
5 tablespoons olive oil
sprig fresh rosemary and thyme
1 large onion, sliced
2 potatoes, diced
10 crushed black peppercorns
¾ teaspoon saffron
1 tablespoon salt
4 slices lemon
1 tablespoon sugar
½ teaspoon paprika
½ teaspoon cayenne
4 large ripe tomatoes
1 cup tomato juice

Remove the meat from the bugs and split lengthways. Scrub the mussels and split the rock lobster in half lengthways and remove the tail. Clean the squid and cut the body into rings. Place the shells or heads from the lobster and bugs in a saucepan with the wine, bouquet garni, and 4 cups water. Bring to a gentle simmer and cook for 20 minutes. Strain the stock through a fine sieve. Heat the oil in a large, heavy saucepan. Add the garlic, thyme, rosemary and onion▶

and saute until translucent. Add the prawns, scallops, lobster tail cut into quarters, and squid. Saute for 3 minutes before adding the potatoes, saffron, peppercorns, salt, lemon, sugar, paprika, and cayenne. Mix the ingredients and add the quartered tomatoes, tomato juice and 3 cups of the strained stock. Simmer gently until the potatoes are tender. Add the mussels and cook until they open. Serve immediately in large bowls (and don't forget the bibs!). *Serves 4.*

crabmeat and mushrooms with 2 tablespoons lemon juice and oil. Place crabmeat in the centre of a serving dish. Cut tomatoes in a bowl. Simmer green capsicum for two minutes in boiling water. Refresh under cold water. Add capsicum and olives to tomatoes. Toss with remaining lemon juice and oil. Drain and arrange around crabmeat. Sprinkle crabmeat with walnuts and parsley. *Serves 4.*

QUEENSLAND MUD CRAB SALAD

1kg (2½lb) Queensland mud crabmeat, cleaned
6 mushrooms, sliced
2 tablespoons lemon juice
6 tablespoons olive oil or vegetable oil
¼ teaspoon salt
black pepper, ground
4 hard boiled eggs
2 tomatoes, cut into wedges
2 green capsicums, cut into strips
12 black olives, pitted
50g (2oz) chopped walnuts
2 tablespoons parsley, chopped

Combine crabmeat and mushrooms in a bowl. Stir together the lemon juice, oil, salt and pepper. Moisten

ROTTNEST ISLAND CRAYFISH MORNAY

500g (1lb) fresh lobster meat
250ml (½pt) white wine
250ml (½pt) milk
½ cup butter or margarine
1 small onion, chopped
1 cup plain flour
salt
cayenne pepper
juice of ½ lemon
1 sliced gherkin
2 tablespoons mayonnaise
1 50g (2oz) egg, beaten
½ cup tasty cheese, grated
2 level tablespoons chopped parsley

1 cup soft breadcrumbs tossed in
1 tablespoon melted butter

Melt butter, saute onion until clear and then add flour, salt and cayenne pepper. cook for about 1 minute. Add the milk and wine, stir constantly until mixture boils and thickens. Add lemon juice, gherkin, mayonnaise, beaten egg, cheese, parsley and flaked lobster. Pour into greased ovenproof dishes and top with buttered breadcrumbs. Sprinkle breadcrumbs with grated tasty cheese and place in a moderate oven 180°C (350°F) to heat through and brown the breadcrumbs. *Serves 4.*

BOTANY BAY MUSSELS

1½kg (3lb) mussels, washed and cleaned
2 tablespoons olive oil
1 tablespoon butter
2 cloves garlic, crushed
1 onion, sliced
½ cup tomato paste
½ teaspoon basil
salt and pepper
1 cup red wine

Make sure the mussels have been cleaned thoroughly and set aside. In a heavy pan, heat the oil and butter and lightly fry the garlic and onion until soft. Add the remaining ingredients and simmer for 10 minutes. Combine the mussels with the sauce. Cover and simmer for 15 minutes or until the shells open. Serve with rice or pasta. Sprinkle with parmesan cheese if desired. *Serves 4-6.*

BBQ WESTERN ROCK LOBSTER

2 uncooked western rock lobsters
½ cup butter
1 clove crushed garlic
⅓ cup chopped fresh dill
¼ cup lemon juice
freshly ground pepper

Split the lobster in half lengthways (allow ½ per person). In a small saucepan, melt the butter and add the remaining ingredients. Brush the mixture on the flesh side of the lobster while cooking. Barbecue or grilling time will depend on the size, 10-12 minutes should be sufficient. Serve on a bed of buttered rice. *Serves 4.*

MEAT

CARPETBAG STEAK

250g (½lb) fillet steak per person
6 Sydney rock oysters per steak
butter
freshly ground black pepper
lemon juice
parsley

Trim fat from meat and cut a pocket into the steak. Fill cavity with oysters and add a squeeze of lemon juice and pepper. Fry in butter, or place on griller until the steak is cooked to your preference. Garnish with parsley butter. *Serves 4.*

STEAK DIANE

6 eye fillet steaks 250g (¼lb per person)
6 cloves garlic
2 tablespoons oil
90g (3oz) butter
3 tablespoons mustard
salt and pepper
8 tablespoons claret
2 tablespoons worcestershire sauce
8 tablespoons cream
8 tablespoons tomato sauce

Crush garlic and mix with oil and a little salt – rub into fillets and allow to stand for 2 hours. Melt butter. Cook steaks for 2 minutes to seal meat, and add salt and pepper to taste. Smear with mustard on sealed side, and cook 2 or 3 minutes on other side. Place steak to one side of pan and add wine and sauces, bring to boil. Stir in cream, but do not boil. *Serves 6.*

GOVERNOR MACQUARIE'S BANQUET ROAST BEEF

1 x 2kg (4½lb) whole topside of beef
¼ cup flour
salt and pepper
½ cup good beef dripping

Rub the meat with the flour and seasonings. Heat the fat in a roasting pan. Place the meat in the pan and brown on all sides. Place the meat on a rack or trivet. Roast in a hot oven at 200°c (400°F) for 10-15 minutes. Reduce the heat to 180°C (375°F) and cook, allowing 20-25 minutes per pound depending on preference. Vegetables such as whole parsnip, pumpkin, carrots and onions can be placed around the meat 45 minutes before the meat is cooked. Baste occasionally. Serve with horseradish sauce and brown gravy. *Serves 6.*

FLAMING ORANGE FILLET

6 eye fillet steaks
fresh pepper
juice of 2 oranges
8 tablespoons brandy
90g (3oz) butter
4 oranges peeled and sliced

Rub steaks with pepper and marinate in orange juice and ½ brandy for 4 hours. Heat butter, drain steaks and cook as desired. Heat orange slices in covered pan. Pour marinade over steaks and heat and garnish. Ignite with remaining brandy. Serve with jacket potatoes and asparagus. *Serves 6.*

DIGGER'S STEAK SANGER

2 x 90g (3oz) lean steak
2 eggs
2 tablespoons oil
1 onion, sliced
1 tomato, sliced
shredded lettuce
2-3 slices beetroot
tomato sauce
4 slices bread

Pound the steak to flatten. Heat the oil and fry the onion until golden; set aside. Fry the steaks and the eggs. Toast the bread and lightly butter. Put the steak on the toast; top with the egg, onion, tomato, lettuce, beetroot slices and tomato sauce. Cut in half diagonally and serve with a cold beer. *Serves 2.*

STEAK AND KIDNEY PUDDING

Suet Crust
150g (5oz) beef suet
250g (8oz) plain flour
½ teaspoon baking powder
½ teaspoon salt
½ cup water

Filling
500g (1lb) round steak, minced
2 kidneys, skinned and finely chopped
1 onion, chopped
2 tablespoons chopped parsley
1 carrot, grated
¼ cup tomato sauce
1 teaspoon salt
½ teaspoon pepper
1 tablespoon curry powder
½ cup stock or water

Skin, flake and chop suet finely. Sift flour, baking powder and salt into a bowl. Rub suet in well with fingertips. Add water gradually, mixing to a dry dough. Turn out onto a floured surface. Divide dough into 2 portions, one larger than the other. Roll each portion thinly and line a well-greased 1 litre sized mould with the larger size. Fill with cold cooked meat filling. Cover with remaining pastry and fork edge. Cover with 2 sheets of greased greaseproof paper and steam for 2 to 2½ hours. When cooked turn out and serve with tomato sauce and vegetables in season. For the filling, place all ingredients into a saucepan. Place lid on saucepan and simmer until meat is cooked. Allow to cool. *Serves 4-6.*

SHEPHERD'S PIE

250g (8oz) mashed potato
500g (1lb) minced lean beef
2 sliced onions
⅓ cup tomato puree
15g (½oz) flour
salt and pepper
30g (1oz) butter
250ml (½pt) beef stock
1 tablespoon worcestershire sauce
extra butter

Lightly fry the onions in the butter. Stir in the flour. Add the stock and stir until the mixture comes to the boil. Remove from the heat and add the meat, seasonings and tomato puree. Cover and simmer for about 20 minutes. Put the meat mixture into an ovenproof dish. Cover with the mashed potato. Dot with extra butter and bake in a hot oven for 20 minutes. Serve with a mixture of garden vegetables. *Serves 4.*

BLUEY'S MEAT ROLL

2 onions, chopped
3 tablespoons butter
2 cups mushrooms, sliced
½ teaspoon garlic salt
½ teaspoon tarragon
2 eggs, beaten
1 cup soft white breadcrumbs
½ cup grated tasty cheese
¾ cup ham, slivered
1 x 5cm (2in) thick slice round steak
cut butterfly fashion
1 teaspoon salt
½ teaspoon pepper
¼ cup sour cream
red paprika powder
parsley, chopped

▶

To butterfly steak, cut a thick piece of steak in half horizontally but not completely through and open out flat. Saute onions in butter until clear. Add mushrooms, salt and tarragon and saute gently about 5 minutes. Meanwhile, combine eggs, breadcrumbs and cheese. Add the ham and sauteed mushroom mixture. Spread the butterfly of steak flat onto a board and pound to make about 1cm (½in) thick and sprinkle with salt and pepper. Spread the mushroom filling over the steak and roll up. Tie up with string at about 4cm (1½in) intervals. Place into a greased baking dish and bake in a moderately hot oven 230°C (450°F) for 15 minutes, then reduce to 190°C (375°F) for further 50 minutes or until meat is tender. Cool and chill. Before serving, remove string and spread with sour cream. Sprinkle with chopped parsley and red paprika. *Serves 4.*

1 tablespoon tomato sauce
oregano
350g (12oz) pkt shortcrust pastry
1 egg

Fry steak and onion in pan until meat is well browned. Pour off excess fat. Add to pan peeled and chopped tomatoes, parsley, sauces, salt, pepper and oregano, and simmer. Cover for 30 minutes and leave to cool. Roll out pastry into 40cm x 20cm (16in x 8in) rectangle, then cut into 10cm (4in) squares. Spoon some of the meat mixture on half of each square, brush edges with a little beaten egg, fold other half of pastry over filling. Seal edges well. Decorate edges, make slit on top with knife to allow steam to escape. Place pastries on tray, brush tops with remaining beaten egg. Bake in hot oven 25 minutes, or until pastry has risen well and is golden brown. *Serves 4.*

MEAT PUFFS

500g (1lb) minced steak
1 onion, chopped
2 tomatoes
1 tablespoon chopped parsley
worcestershire sauce
salt and pepper

BEEF AND SPICY COCONUT

500g (1lb) beef topside steak
8 shallots
3cm (1½in) fresh ginger
20 dried red chillies, soaked
2 stalks lemon grass
1 garlic clove

6 tablespoons freshly grated coconut
or 4 tablespoons desiccated coconut
3 tablespoons oil
2½ cups coconut milk
1 leaf fresh tumeric, very finely shredded
1 teaspoon salt
1 teaspoon sugar

Cut beef into pieces about 5cm (2in) and 1cm (½in) thick. Grind the shallots, ginger, chillies, lemon grass and garlic together until fine. Gently fry the grated coconut in a dry pan, stirring constantly, until golden brown. Allow to cool slightly, and pound to a paste. Heat oil and gently fry the ground shallot mixture for 4-5 minutes. Add pounded coconut and fry for another minute. Add beef and stir-fry until it changes colour. Add all other ingredients and stir, lifting the coconut milk and pouring it back, until it comes to the boil. Reduce heat and simmer, uncovered, until the meat is tender. The sauce should finally reduce so that all that remains is a very thick coating on the steak. *Serves 4.*

SWAGGIES' BEEF HOT POT

1½kg (3½lb) gravy beef, diced
1 litre (1½pt) stock or water
1kg (2lb) shelled peas

4 carrots, diced
2 small turnips, diced
12 small onions
500g (1lb) broad beans
1 teaspoon mixed herbs
1 cup chopped parsley

Put the meat in a heavy casserole dish. Cover with the stock and bring to the boil and stir occasionally. Add the vegetables and herbs to the soup. Lower the heat and simmer for 3-4 hours. Add the parsley before serving. The soup should be very thick. This dish can be accompanied by dumplings if desired. *Serves 6.*

MINCED BEEF AND OKRA LOAF

1.5kg (3lb) fresh okra, washed
1½ tablespoons butter, melted
1 onion, finely chopped
1kg (2lb) minced topside steak
1½ tablespoons flour
1 teaspoon prepared crushed garlic
4 tablespoons tomato paste
2 teaspoons salt
freshly ground black pepper
1¼ cups beef stock

▶

Trim end of okra, saute 4 minutes in butter. Remove from pan, drain well. Saute onion and meat in butter till brown. Add remaining ingredients using only ¾ cup of stock. Cook quickly till thickened. Remove from heat. Firmly press half meat mixture into well greased 20cm (8in) round deep cake tin. Layer okra in a spoke-like pattern – cut edges out, on top of meat. Press remaining meat on top. Drizzle with remaining stock. Bake in moderately slow oven 180°C (350°F) for 1 hour. Allow to stand in tin 5 minutes. Loosen edges and invert onto serving platter. Serve garnished with lemon wedges. *Serves 6.*

CORNED BEEF AND CABBAGE

2kg (4lb) corned beef
2 sliced carrots
3 onions, 1 stuck with 4 cloves
1 cabbage, large
1 teaspoon dry mustard powder
thyme sprig
parsley sprig
pepper
water

Put the meat into a large saucepan with all ingredients except the cabbage. Cover with water and bring to the boil. Skim off any scum. Cover and simmer very gently for ¾ hour. Put in the cabbage, trimmed and cut into quarters. Cook the meat for 2 hours and serve on a dish garnished with the cabbage. *Serves 6.*

OLD FASHIONED MEAT PIE

500g (1lb) rich short crust pastry

Filling
1kg (2lb) topside steak, cubed
flour, salt and pepper
2-3 tablespoons oil
2 onions, chopped
¼ teaspoon nutmeg
2 teaspoons worcestershire sauce
2½ cups beef stock

Toss the meat in the seasoned flour. Heat the oil and brown the meat pieces. Remove and drain. Add the onions to the pan and soften. Stir in the nutmeg and 2 tablespoons of the seasoned flour. Pour on the stock and the sauce. Stir well. Return the meat. Cover and simmer for 1 hour. Cool. Roll half the pastry to fit a 23cm (8in) pie dish, line with the pastry. Spoon in the meat mixture. Roll the remaining pastry and place on top of the pie. Crimp the edges and make 2-3 slashes in the lid. Brush with a little milk. Bake for 25-35 minutes at 180°C (350°F). Serve with steamed vegetables. *Serves 6.*

GOVERNOR'S PLEASURE

60g (3oz) olive oil
1½kg (3lb) beef, chuck or blade
2 garlic cloves
2 bay leaves
2 tablespoons paprika
1 500g (1lb) can beef consomme
150ml (5 fl oz) red wine
1kg (2lb) small new potatoes
200g (6oz) button mushrooms

Cut beef into cubes. Saute in hot oil with crushed garlic and paprika. Transfer to a large saucepan. Add bay leaves, soup and wine. Cover and simmer gently for ¾ hour. Add peeled whole potatoes and simmer ½ hour, covered. Add mushrooms and cook 20 minutes without lid. *Serves 6.*

TRIPE IN WINE SAUCE

750g (1½lb) tripe
600ml (1pt) water
¾ cup dry white wine
2 chicken stock cubes
2 medium carrots
2 medium onions
parsley, chopped
salt and pepper

Cut blanched tripe into strips. Place in saucepan with water, wine, and crumbled stock cubes. Bring to boil. Reduce heat, simmer, covered, 2 hours. Add chopped onions and sliced carrots. Cook further 30 minutes or until tender. Add chopped parsley and season to taste with salt and pepper. *Serves 4.*

OX TONGUE WITH RAISIN SAUCE

1 fresh ox tongue
2 carrots, diced
2 onions, diced
1 stick celery, chopped
½ cup chopped parsley
6 cloves
salt and pepper

Put the tongue, vegetables, parsley, cloves, salt and pepper into a saucepan. Cover with cold water and bring to the boil. Cover and simmer for 2½-3 hours. Remove from the stock and trim off the excess fat, gristle and skin. Slice thinly and place on a serving dish. Cover with foil and keep warm in the oven. *Serves 4.*

Raisin Sauce
2 tablespoons butter
2 tablespoons flour
1 cup beef stock
1 cup white wine
1 cup raisins soaked in
½ cup port
½ teaspoon nutmeg
grated rind of 1 lemon
¾ cup blanched almonds

Melt the butter and stir in the flour, stirring constantly. Gradually add the stock, wine, almonds and raisins with the port. Add the lemon rind and the nutmeg. Simmer for 20 minutes. Adjust the seasonings and spoon over the tongue. Serve with boiled potatoes and garden vegetables.

MAMA'S VEAL

3 tablespoons plain flour
2 teaspoons salt
¾ teaspoon pepper
1kg (2½lb) veal fillets or steak
cut into thin slices
4 tablespoons butter or margarine
2 peeled cloves of garlic

2 medium onion, sliced
1kg (2lb) tin tomato puree
3 tablespoons brown sugar
1 cup stock
1 teaspoon mixed herbs
⅓ cup sherry
250g (½lb) mushrooms
parmesan cheese

Combine the flour, salt and pepper and coat the veal. Keep the remaining flour for thickening later. Heat the butter or margarine in a deep frying pan and brown the veal, garlic and the onions. Remove veal and onions and discard the garlic. Simmer tomato puree, brown sugar, stock and herbs together for about 5 minutes. Return the veal and onions to this sauce. Cover and cook slowly for 40 minutes. When the meat is tender, thicken the sauce with the blended seasoned flour, if necessary. Add the sherry and mushrooms if desired. Serve sprinkled with cheese, accompanied by small buttered pasta. *Serves 6.*

VEAL POT ROAST

2kg (4½lb) boneless veal roast
1 tablespoon dry mustard powder

2 tablespoons soft brown sugar
1 tablespoon salt
1 tablespoon flour
2 tablespoons vegetable oil
1 445g (15oz) can vegetable soup
½ cup water

Coat veal roast with mixture of mustard powder, brown sugar, salt and flour. In large covered fry pan or heavy saucepan, brown the roast in oil. Pour vegetable soup over the roast, cover and simmer 2 hours. Add water during cooking if required. *Serves 6.*

LAMB'S FRY AND BACON

250g (½lb) bacon
1 lamb's fry
1 tablespoon plain flour
salt and pepper
2 onions, sliced
1 apple, sliced
1 teaspoon sugar
1 cup light stock
1 cup cider
125g (¼lb) fresh white breadcrumbs
25g (1oz) bacon fat

Trim rind from the bacon. Cut into bite-sized pieces and fry lightly. Wash and slice the liver, coat in seasoned flour and place in a shallow casserole. Drain bacon, scatter on top of liver. Add onions and apple and sprinkle on sugar. Pour over the stock and cider. Heat one tablespoon of fat in the pan, add breadcrumbs and stir through. Spread crumbs over casserole, cover and bake at 190°C (375°F) for 45 minutes. Uncover, and cook 10 minutes to crisp the top. *Serves 4.*

SPICED LAMB SHANKS

4 lamb shanks
2 tablespoons flour
3 tablespoons oil
1 onion, sliced
1 x 450g (15oz) can tomato soup
¼ cup vinegar
½ cup tomato sauce
1 tablespoon worcestershire sauce

Coat shanks with flour. Brown in oil with onion. Remove to casserole. Add remaining ingredients to pan and bring to the boil stirring constantly. Pour sauce over shanks and onion. Cover and bake at 180°C (350°F) for 1½ hours, stirring occasionally. *Serves 4.*

MUTTON CHOPS IN A BLANKET

8 shortloin mutton chops
350g (12oz) mushrooms, finely chopped
3 slices ham
1 large onion
120g (4oz) butter
dash worcestershire sauce
salt and pepper
2 pkts puff pastry
egg

Bone and trim chops. Wrap tail around to form circle. Secure with toothpick. Saute in a little butter until golden. Drain. Add remaining butter, saute mushrooms, ham and onion, season. Roll out pastry cut into 8 circles to encase each chop. Glaze edges with egg. Spread mushroom mixture on each side of chops. Place on pastry, seal, glaze with egg and prick. Bake in hot oven 200°C (400°F) 15-20 minutes until golden brown. *Serves 4.*

SQUATTER'S HOT POT

16 best neck lamb chops
8 tomatoes
8 onions

8 potatoes
2 parsnips
4 carrots
plain flour
salt and pepper
beef stock
4 cups breadcrumbs

Trim fat off the chops and place in a large greased aluminium baking dish with cover, or a large oven-proof dish (if no lid cover with foil). Sprinkle well with plain flour, pepper and salt. Slice tomatoes evenly over each chop. Slice the onions over tomatoes and peel potatoes, parsnips and carrots. Slice very thinly and evenly over the onions. Pour enough stock into the dish to come up to the top of the chops only. Cover dish and bake in a moderate oven for 1 hour. Remove the cover. Sprinkle heavily with breadcrumbs and bake uncovered for a further ½ hour, until potatoes and crumbs are golden and crisp on top. Serve with boiled potatoes. *Serves 4-6.*

LAMB NOISETTES WITH MINT BUTTER

8 noisettes of lamb
120g (4oz) butter or substitute
2 tablespoons chopped mint

flour
salt and pepper
melted butter
8 slices bread

Buy lamb chops 1½ to 2½cm (¾in to 1in) thick. Ask butcher to prepare them as noisettes. Roll chops in flour which has been seasoned with salt and pepper. Brush with a little melted butter. Place in greased baking dish. Bake in moderate oven approximately 30 minutes, or until brown and tender, turning once. Toast 8 slices of bread. Cut toast into circles. Top each toast circle with a noisette. Put a pat of mint butter on top of each. Serve with green peas and pommes parisienne. *Serves 4.*

Mint Butter

Chop mint very finely. Mix with softened butter. Refrigerate until firm.

COLONIAL GOOSE

1 x 1½kg (3lb) boned leg of lamb
Stuffing
90g (3oz) chopped bacon
½ tablespoon chopped parsley
1 medium onion, chopped
1 teaspoon mixed herbs
½ teaspoon nutmeg
½ teaspoon grated lemon rind
salt and pepper
1 egg, beaten
milk

Combine all the ingredients, adding enough milk and egg to bind the mixture. Stuff into the cavity of the leg and tie securely. Heat a little fat in a roasting pan and brown the meat on all sides. Roast at 200°C (400°F) for 15 minutes. Reduce to 180°C (350°F) for 1½ hours or until desired. To serve, remove the string and place on a meat platter surrounded by whole baby new potatoes, carrots and acorn squash. Make a brown gravy from the pan juices. *Serves 4.*

Brown Gravy

2 tablespoons flour
250ml (½pt) beef stock
salt and pepper

Remove most of the excess fat from the roasting pan leaving the scrapings and approximately 2 tablespoons of fat. Heat on top of the stove. Add the flour and cook slowly to brown. Remove from the stove and slowly pour on the stock, stirring constantly. Return to stove and bring to the boil. Season with salt and pepper.

CRUMBED LAMB CUTLETS

8 lamb cutlets
1 egg
1 tablespoon milk
2 tablespoons flour
1 teaspoon salt
½ teaspoon pepper
¾ cup dry breadcrumbs

Remove skin and gristle from cutlets, but do not remove fat. Beat egg in a bowl, add milk. Mix flour, salt and pepper on greaseproof paper. Place breadcrumbs on second piece greaseproof paper. Dredge cutlets in flour, salt and pepper. Dip in beaten egg and milk, toss in breadcrumbs. Firm crumbs on with a broad-bladed knife and reshape cutlets. Heat a small quantity of fat in frying pan. Add cutlets and shallow fry quickly for 1 minute on each side. Reduce heat and cook gently for 10 minutes, turning when necessary. Drain cutlets on paper towel. Serve with creamed, mashed potatoes, vegetables in season and mint sauce. *Serves 4.*

SHEARER'S BRAWN

1 veal knuckle
½ pig cheek

500g (1lb) chuck steak
1 cup chopped parsley
½ teaspoon thyme
½ teaspoon marjoram
¼ teaspoon sage
2 bay leaves
6 peppercorns
½ teaspoon allspice
cold water
2 tablespoons gelatine

Place the meats in a large saucepan with the herbs, spices and enough water to cover. Bring slowly to the boil; skim occasionally. Simmer for 3-4 hours. Remove the meats from the stock and shred. Discard the bones and gristle. Pack the meat into a loaf tin or terrine dish. Bring the remaining stock to the boil and reduce; add the gelatine and strain over the meat. Cool and refrigerate for 24 hours. Serve with tossed salad. *Serves 6.*

BANGERS AND MASH

8 thick pork sausages
6 potatoes, peel and quartered

¼ cup milk
2 tablespoons butter
pinch nutmeg
½ teaspoon salt
freshly ground black pepper
1 onion, sliced into rings
oil

Cook the potatoes in boiling water for 15 minutes, drain and mash with the butter, milk and seasonings. Keep warm. Prick the sausages and grill for 10-12 minutes on both sides. Meanwhile fry the onion rings in little oil until golden brown. To serve pile the mashed potato onto a plate with the sausages and top with the onions. This dish is usually accompanied by tomato and worcestershire sauce. *Serves 4.*

BILLABONG BAKED CHEERIOS AND APPLES

1kg (2½lb) cheerios or cocktail franks
3 tablespoons french mustard
2 large Granny Smith (green) apples,
peeled and sliced
2 tablespoons brown sugar

1 cup cider
1 tablespoon butter

Put the sausages into a shallow baking dish and spread the mustard over them. Top with the sliced apples. Mix the sugar with the cider and pour on. Place nuts of butter on the apples. Bake 180°C (350°F) for 25-30 minutes or until the apples are golden brown. *Serves 4.*

CRACKLY ROAST PORK

1 leg of pork, approximately 2.5kg (5lb)
salt
½ cup oil

Ask the butcher to score the rind as this will ensure crisp crackle. Rub the rind generously with salt and brush with the oil. Place on a rack in a roasting pan and roast at 230°C (450°F) for 30 minutes. Reduce the heat to 170°C (350°F) and cook for 2½ hours or until cooked. Baste frequently. Remove from the oven and lift the crackling off, carve into thin slices and serve with sliced roast pork, apple sauce, brown gravy and baked vegetables. *Serves 6-8.*

PORK CHOPS WITH ROSEMARY

4 pork loin chops
30g (1oz) butter
salt and
pepper
1 clove garlic
1 teaspoon dried rosemary
1 tablespoon flour
1 teaspoon vinegar
1 cup water

Trim excess fat from chops. Heat butter in pan, brown chops on both sides. Add salt, pepper, crushed garlic and rosemary. Cook 5 minutes. Add flour, stir well to combine, cook 1 minute. Remove from heat, bring to boil, stirring until mixture boils and thickens. Reduce heat, cover, and simmer gently for approximately 15 minutes. *Serves 4.*

ROAST LOIN OF PORK WITH PRUNE AND PORT SAUCE

1 loin of pork (8 chops)
lemon
1 tablespoon flour
300ml (10 fl oz) water
salt and pepper
Prune and Port Sauce
120g (4oz) prunes
4 tablespoons port wine
water
2 teaspoons lemon juice

Score pork rind well. Trim any excess fat from meat, rub skin with salt, then sprinkle with lemon juice. Put in oiled baking dish, roast in hot oven 20 minutes, then reduce heat to moderate. Continue cooking until meat is well browned and tender. Allow 25 to 30 minutes per 500g (1lb) cooking time. Remove from pan. Keep warm. Pour off pan drippings leaving 1 tablespoon. Add flour, cook 1 minute, stirring gradually. Add water, stir until sauce boils. Season with salt and pepper, then strain into prune mixture. *Serves 4.*

Prune and Port Sauce

Put prunes in small saucepan. Add 3 tablespoons of port and enough water barely to cover prunes. Simmer on low heat, uncovered, until tender. Cool, remove stones from prunes and puree. Add remaining port and lemon juice. Add any liquid remaining from cooking the prunes. Add strained gravy. Heat through gently. Spoon over each serving.

POULTRY & GAME

CHINA'S CHICKEN WINGS

1kg (2lb) chicken wings
½ cup soy sauce
½ cup dry sherry
1 tablespoon sesame oil
25cm (10in) sliced ginger, chopped
2 cloves garlic, chopped
2 tablespoons oil

Combine all the ingredients and marinate the chicken wings overnight. Place the wings in a baking dish with the marinade. Bake at 180°C (350°F) for 30-40 minutes. Serve hot or cold. *Serves 6.*

PINEAPPLE GLAZED CHICKEN

No. 14, 1.4kg (2½lb) roasting chicken
plain flour
60g (2oz) butter
2 teaspoons salad oil
½ cup chopped onion
½ cup chopped celery
½ cup chicken stock
450g (15oz) can unsweetened pineapple
(drain, reserve liquid)
½ teaspoon marjoram
2 teaspoons salt
12 black olives
1 teaspoon cornflour
little water

Dust chicken with flour. Heat oil and butter in fry pan. Add chicken and fry until brown and crisp all over. Transfer to large casserole dish and fry chopped onion and celery in fry pan, add to casserole. Then add stock, reserved pineapple liquid, marjoram and salt. Cover and cook for 1½ hours or until chicken is just tender. Remove lid, raise heat to 200°C (400°F) and cook further ½ hour, or until breast is golden brown. Transfer to serving dish, keep warm. Strain juices into saucepan, add 6 olives. Bring to boil, thicken with cornflour mixed with water. Pour into gravy boat. Grill pineapple slices, remaining olives and vegetables. *Serves 4.*

CHICKEN SUPREME CASSEROLE

¼ cup butter (or margarine)
¼ cup plain flour
¼ teaspoon each of rosemary, oregano
and marjoram
1 cup chicken broth
¼ cup cream

2-3 cups cooked chopped chicken
60g (2oz) extra butter
¼ cup grated cheddar cheese
pinch paprika

In a saucepan melt the butter. Blend in the flour and herbs. Gradually stir in the broth. Cook, stirring constantly until the mixture thickens. Add the cooked chicken. Remove from heat and stir in the cream. Pour into a casserole dish. Dot with butter and sprinkle with the cheese and paprika. Serve when heated through and the cheese is melted. *Serves 4.*

VINEYARD CHICKEN

1½ tablespoons butter
1 tablespoon oil
125g (4oz) salt pork, ham or bacon, chopped
12 small onions
1-2 cloves garlic, crushed
3 cups button mushrooms
1 x 1½kg (3lb) chicken, jointed
½ cup seasoned flour
2 bay leaves
¾ teaspoon salt
black pepper, freshly ground

½ teaspoon thyme
2 parsley sprigs
¼ cup brandy
400ml (13 fl oz) red wine
1 teaspoon sugar
2 teaspoons flour
¼ cup finely chopped parsley

Heat butter and oil in pan, fry pork, onions, garlic. Add mushrooms, fry gently, remove ingredients from pan. Dredge chicken pieces in seasoned flour, saute in pan for 5-10 minutes till well browned, use extra butter if necessary. Return mushrooms, onions and pork to pan, add next 5 ingredients. Cover and cook over low heat 20-30 minutes. Warm brandy, ignite, add to pan. Allow to burn 1 minute then extinguish by pouring in red wine, add sugar. Blend flour with some of the liquid, add to dish, stir till thickened. Serve hot, garnished with finely chopped parsley and mashed potatoes. *Serves 6.*

ROAST SPRING CHICKEN WITH PICKLED WALNUT AND RAISIN STUFFING

1 x 1½kg (3lb) chicken
90g (3oz) butter

▶

1 onion, chopped
½ cup parsley chopped
½ cup raisins
1 cup pickled walnuts, chopped
2 cups cooked wild rice
freshly ground black pepper
salt
125g (4oz) melted butter
1 cup white wine

To prepare the stuffing melt the butter and saute the onion. Add the remaining ingredients and cook for 2-3 minutes. Fill the cavity of the chicken and truss. Season the chicken with salt and pepper and brush with the melted butter. Roast at 180°C (350°F) for 1½ hours. Baste frequently. When the chicken is cooked, remove it from the pan. Pour the wine and stir to lift the pan scrapings. Reduce by ⅓, strain and serve with the roast. *Serves 4-6.*

CHICKEN BREASTS WITH PORT WINE SAUCE

**2 whole chicken breasts
(skinned and boned)**

plain flour
1 egg
1¼ cups finely chopped blanched almonds
3 tablespoons butter
1 tablespoon water
salt
pepper

Sprinkle the chicken with salt and pepper. Coat with flour. Beat the egg lightly with the water. Dip the chicken pieces in the egg mixture and coat with the blanched almonds. Fry in the butter over low to moderate heat, turning chicken over once. Allow 10 minutes each side. Serve with the sauce. *Serves 6-8.*

Port Wine Sauce

1 cup port wine
3 tablespoons finely chopped shallots
1 tablespoon each of
lemon and orange juice
½ teaspoon each grated
lemon and orange rind
¼ teaspoon pepper
pinch each of thyme
salt and cayenne

Port Wine Sauce

Combine port wine, shallots, lemon and orange juice and rind, pepper, salt, thyme and cayenne in a saucepan. Cook over high heat until reduced by a half. Strain into 1 cup Veloute sauce *(see page 62)* and keep warm.

HOMESTEAD CHICKEN PIE

4 cups cooked diced chicken
2 tablespoons butter
1 onion, chopped
2 sticks celery, chopped
2 carrots, diced
½ cup frozen peas
½ cup whole kernel corn
1 potato, diced
½ teaspoon mixed herbs
salt and
pepper
2 tablespoons flour
1 cup chicken stock
120g (4oz) button mushrooms, washed
½ cup cream
puff pastry
beaten egg

Melt the butter and add the onion, celery, carrots, peas, corn and potatoes; cook for 2-3 minutes. Add the seasonings and flour. Cook for 2 minutes stirring constantly. Pour on the chicken stock and bring to the boil, then simmer for another 2 minutes. Stir in the chicken, mushrooms and cream. Pour the mixture into a greased, deep pie dish and cook. Roll out the pastry allowing an extra 2.5cm (1in) around the edge. Place on top of the chicken, pinch the edge and make an air vent in the top. Glaze with a little beaten egg. Bake at 200°C (400°F) for 10 minutes, reduce to 180°C (350°F) for 30-35 minutes. *Serves 6.*

PIGEON CASSEROLE

60g (2oz) butter
125g (4oz) smoked pork, diced
250g (8oz) baby onions
4 pigeons
125g (4oz) button mushrooms
45g (1½oz) flour
1 bay leaf
180ml (6 fl oz) apple cider
500ml (1pt) chicken stock
salt and
pepper

▶

Melt the butter and lightly fry the diced pork, then drain. Add the onions and lightly brown, remove and drain. Brown the pigeons all over, then drain. Add the mushrooms and put aside. Add the flour, stir well to lift the scrapings from the pan. Pour in the cider and stock. Bring to the boil and simmer for 10 minutes. Place the pigeons, pork, vegetables and bay leaf in a casserole dish. Pour the sauce over and cover with a lid. Bake in a moderate oven for approximately 2 hours. Serve with suet dumplings and green vegetables. *Serves 4.*

ROAST DUCKLING WITH FIGS

1 x 2kg (4½lb) duckling
1 cup chicken stock
1 onion
500g (1lb) dried figs, sliced
250ml (8 fl oz) rummy port
salt and pepper

Macerate the figs in the port for 3-4 hours, then prepare the duck for roasting in the usual manner. Season with salt and pepper and place an onion in the cavity. Stand on a rack or trivet over the stock and roast in a hot oven for 1 hour. Remove from the oven and combine the pan juices and port. Reserve the figs. Reduce the liquid by one third, add the sliced figs and cook for 5 minutes. Divide the duck into serving-size pieces and garnish with the figs and sauce. *Serves 4-6.*

ROAST TURKEY WITH STUFFING

1 x 5kg (10lb) turkey
2 tablespoons butter or margarine, softened
1 teaspoon salt
freshly ground black pepper
1 teaspoon paprika

Stuffing

1kg (2lb) sausage meat
2 tablespoons butter
2 medium sized onions, finely chopped
2 stalks celery, finely chopped
1 cup walnuts, chopped
Turkey liver, chopped
4 tablespoons finely chopped parsley
1 teaspoon salt
freshly ground black pepper
2 cups breadcrumbs,
freshly made
3 eggs, lightly beaten

Giblet Gravy

giblets from turkey
2 onions, finely chopped
2 stalks celery, stems and leaves
1 bay leaf

3 sprigs parsley
½ teaspoon salt
1 cup white wine
1½ cups chicken stock
3 tablespoons butter
3 tablespoons flour
1 teaspoon peppercorns

To prepare the stuffing: Fry sausage meat and pour off excess fat. Place sausage meat in a bowl. Heat the butter and fry the onions, celery, nuts and turkey liver for 5 minutes over moderate heat. Add these ingredients to the sausage. Stir in all the remaining ingredients and fill into the turkey cavity. Secure dressing with poultry skewers. Rub outside skin of the turkey with softened butter. Season with salt, pepper and paprika. Place the turkey on a rack in a baking dish. Roast uncovered in a 160°C (325°F) oven for 3½ hours. (Allow 30 minutes additional time for each extra kg of turkey). Place giblets, onions, celery, bay leaf, parsley, salt, pepper, wine and stock in a saucepan. Cover and simmer over very low heat for 1½ hours. Strain the stock. When the turkey has cooked, skim the fat from the juices in the baking dish. Pour the liquid into the stock. Add butter to melt. Stir in the flour. Add ½ cup cold chicken stock and scrape up the pan scrapings. Add reserved strained chicken stock. Stir to form a smooth gravy. *Serves 8.*

RABBIT PIE

750g (1½lb) rabbit meat, boned
500ml (1pt) chicken stock
1 cup dry white wine
1 onion, diced
1 parsnip, diced
2 carrots, diced
2 potatoes, diced
1 tablespoon oil
2 tablespoons flour
1 teaspoon mixed dried herbs
3 cloves garlic, crushed
salt and pepper
1 pkt prepared puff pastry

Chop rabbit meat into small chunks and toss in seasoned flour. Saute in oil until lightly browned. Place in deep pie dish or casserole with the vegetables. Cover with chicken stock. Add white wine, herbs, garlic and bring to boil. Simmer gently until meat and vegetables are tender. Thicken, if desired, with cornflour. Put aside until cold, transfer to a pie dish. Roll out pastry as directed on packet and place over rabbit mixture. Trim edges and use excess pastry to decorate – make two or three slits in top. Brush lightly with beaten egg and place in oven as directed for puff pastry. *Serves 4.*

PASTA, VEGETABLES & SALADS

BUBBLE AND SQUEAK

3 tablespoons butter
1 small onion, finely chopped
2 cups shredded cabbage, cooked
2 cups potatoes, mashed

Heat the butter in a frying pan and fry the onion over low heat for 5 minutes until softened. Add cabbage and stir over low heat for 2 minutes. Fold in the mashed potatoes until well blended with the cabbage. Press mixture lightly onto the surface of the pan to form a large pancake. Cook for 5 minutes until the underside has browned lightly. Turn and brown on the second side for five minutes. *Serves 4.*

SPINACH CROQUETTES

1 bunch spinach or silverbeet
2 hard boiled eggs
1 onion, grated
salt and pepper
½ teaspoon nutmeg
plain flour
beaten eggs
dry breadcrumbs
oil

Wash and chop the spinach and cook for 5-6 minutes. Remove from the stove and press gently to remove excess liquid. Mix in the hard boiled egg, onion and seasonings. Shape into walnut size balls. Dip in flour, beaten egg and breadcrumbs. Deep fry in hot oil, drain and serve. *Serves 4.*

STUFFED PARSNIPS

6 parsnips
1½ cups fresh white breadcrumbs
1 small onion, chopped
1 tablespoon butter
2 tablespoons mixed herbs
1 tablespoon chopped parsley
salt and pepper
1 egg, beaten
melted butter

Wash and peel the parsnips and cut in half, lengthwise. Carefully remove the centre core. Place in cold water while preparing the stuffing. Melt the butter and lightly fry the onion. Combine all the remaining ingredients and place spoonsful of the mixture along each half of the parsnip. Brush with melted butter. The parsnip can be placed around a roasting meat or baked in a separate greased dish for 20-30 minutes. *Serves 4-6.*

YORKSHIRE PUDDING

1 cup milk
2 eggs
1 cup plain flour
3 tablespoons hot oil
1 teaspoon salt

Place the milk, eggs, flour, salt and 2 tablespoons hot fat in a blender and blend until smooth. Pour 1 table-spoon fat into a 23cm (8in) pie plate. Pour in the bat-ter. Bake in a 220°C (450°F) oven for 15 minutes. Reduce the heat to 180°C (350°F) and continue cooking for another 15 minutes until the pudding is puffed and a crisp brown. Cut into wedges and serve immediately with roast beef. *Serves 4.*

SPAGHETTI NINO CULOTTA

2 tablespoons olive oil
1 small onion
500g (1lb) veal and pork mince
60g (2oz) Italian salami
125g (4oz) ham pieces
salt and pepper
1 teaspoon basil
500g (1lb) ripe tomatoes
1 cup red wine
375g (12oz) spaghetti
30g (1oz) grated pecorino or parmesan cheese

Heat oil in pan, add peeled and finely chopped onion, veal and pork mince, chopped salami and finely chop-ped ham pieces. Fry until golden brown, breaking up meat. Add salt, pepper, basil, peeled and chopped tomatoes and red wine, stir until combined. Simmer gently, uncovered, for 2 hours; add more wine if desired. Boil spaghetti as directed on packet, then drain. Layer sauce and spaghetti in serving dish, sprinkle with parmesan cheese and bake at 180°C (350°F) for 25 minutes. *Serves 4.*

BRUSSELS SPROUTS WITH WINE AND RAISINS

⅔ cup seedless raisins
1kg (2lb) partly cooked sprouts
2 tablespoons butter
⅔ cup dry white wine
pinch of pepper and nutmeg

Combine raisins and wine. Let stand 1 hour, then com-bine brussels sprouts, seasonings and butter and finish cooking over very low heat for 5 minutes. *Serves 6.*

SUET DUMPLINGS

180g (6oz) flour
1 teaspoon baking powder
90g (3oz) grated suet
pinch salt
½ cup cold water

Sift the flour, baking powder and salt, and mix in the suet. Gradually add enough water to form a soft dough. Shape into small balls about the size of a walnut. If you wish, cook the dumplings in the gravy with the meat you are serving or drop into boiling water and cook for 10-15 minutes. *Serves 4*

MACARONI CHEESE

250g (8oz) mararoni, cooked
½ cup butter
⅓ cup flour
salt and pepper to taste
1 teaspoon mustard
pinch paprika
1⅔ cups milk
250g (8oz) finely grated cheese
1 medium can tomato soup
4 rashers bacon, chopped

1 onion, chopped
2 tablespoons capsicum, chopped
1 tablespoon worcestershire sauce
thin slices of cheese
tomato slices

Melt butter in saucepan and add flour and seasonings. Cook 1 minute. Add milk, stirring over heat until sauce boils and thickens. Add cheese and tomato puree to sauce. Reheat gently but do not boil. Fry bacon, onion and capsicum lightly and add to sauce. Add worcestershire sauce and macaroni. Place in a greased, ovenproof dish and place cheese and tomato slices alternately around the edge of the dish. Bake in a moderate oven 180°C (350°F) for 25 minutes. *Serves 4.*

CURRIED VEGETABLES

1 large onion, chopped
1 large potato, diced
½ small cabbage
¼ small cauliflower
3 carrots, diced
250g (½lb) green beans, sliced
¼ cup vegetable oil
2 cloves crushed garlic
1 tablespoon chopped ginger

▶

2 tablespoons curry powder
1 cup coconut milk
salt

Lightly fry the onion and garlic, add the ginger and curry powder. Add the potato and cook for 1 minute. Combine the remaining ingredients, cover and simmer for 20 minutes. *Serves 4.*

CLAPSHOT

500g (1lb) potatoes
250g (½lb) turnips
60g (2oz) butter
2 tablespoons chopped mint
salt and pepper

Cook the vegetables in boiling, salted water. Drain and mash with the butter, salt, pepper and mint. Serve with corned beef. *Serves 6.*

CREAMED MUSHROOMS

500g (1lb) field mushrooms
1 onion, chopped
60g (2oz) butter

salt and pepper
½ cup sour cream
2 tablespoons chopped parsley

Clean and slice the mushrooms. Melt the butter and fry the onion until soft. Add the mushrooms and cook for 5-6 minutes. Stir in the sour cream, salt and pepper. Sprinkle with chopped parsley. Serve with grilled or barbecued steak. *Serves 4.*

MARINATED MUSHROOMS

500g (1lb) large mushrooms
lemon slices
½ cup olive oil
salt and pepper
1 clove garlic
½ cup coarsely grated parmesan cheese

Choose fresh, firm mushrooms. Scrape any traces of soil from the mushrooms, clean and wipe them with a damp cloth, then rub them with slices of lemon. Do not cut off the stems. Season in a serving dish with a mixture of oil, salt, pepper and a drop of garlic pressed from a garlic press. Sprinkle with grated parmesan cheese. Serve this raw mushroom salad as a vegetable, to accompany cold dishes. *Serves 4.*

SWEET POTATO CROQUETTES

2 cups mashed sweet potato
60g (2oz) butter
1 egg yolk for binding
salt and pepper
2 teaspoons grated lemon zest
beaten egg
breadcrumbs

Combine the butter, potato, lemon zest, salt and pepper. Roll into cylindrical shapes. Dip in beaten egg and breadcrumbs. Chill well. Deep fry until golden brown, drain and serve hot. *Serves 4-6.*

BRAISED PEAS

500g (½lb) fresh peas
2 rashers bacon, diced
1 tablespoon butter
1 onion, finely chopped
1 clove garlic, crushed
¼ cup tomato paste
½ cup white wine
salt and pepper

Lightly fry the bacon, onion and garlic until soft. Add the peas, tomato paste, wine and seasonings. Cover and simmer for 20 minutes. *Serves 4.*

MURPHY'S COLCANNON

6-8 potatoes, peeled and quartered
½ cabbage, shredded
4-6 chopped shallots
300ml (10 fl oz) milk
½ cup butter
2 tablespoons butter
salt and pepper

Cook the potatoes in boiling water until tender, drain and set aside. Cook the cabbage in boiling water for 5-7 minutes then drain. Mash the potato with the milk and add the remaining ingredients. Serve hot. *Serves 4-6.*

GINGERED BUTTERNUT PUMPKIN

750g (¾lb) pumpkin
½ cup butter
⅓ cup brown sugar
½ cup preserved ginger in syrup

▶

Cut the pumpkin into 8cm (3in) pieces. Blanch in boiling water for 2 minutes, drain and run under cold water to prevent further cooking. Melt the butter, add the sugar and the ginger. Place the pumpkin in an oven to table dish and pour the ginger mixture over it. Bake at 180°C (350°F) for 30-35 minutes. Serve with roast or barbecue meats. Note – Sweet potato or yams can be used instead of pumpkin, if preferred. *Serves 4-6.*

CAIRNS COLESLAW

½ firm, white cabbage
1 cup grated carrot
1 cup celery, finely chopped
1 onion, finely chopped
1 Granny Smith (green) apple, chopped
1 cup pineapple, chopped
1 green capsicum, finely chopped
½ cup mayonnaise, homemade
salt and pepper
lemon juice or cider vinegar (optional)

Wash and shred the cabbage. Put all the ingredients in a salad bowl and mix thoroughly. A little lemon juice or cider vinegar can be added if a sharper flavour is preferred. Serve with cold or barbecued meats. *Serves 6-8.*

WATERCRESS SALAD

1 bunch watercress
6 shallots
2 oranges
½ cup French dressing
1 cup black olives
½ cup walnuts

Wash and dry the watercress, chill. Chop the shallots and thinly slice the peeled oranges. Toss all ingredients and serve. *Serves 4.*

RED CABBAGE SALAD

½ red cabbage, shredded
1 large onion, finely chopped
1 large red apple, finely chopped
2 tablespoons cider vinegar
4 tablespoons oil
2 teaspoons sugar
1 tablespoon caraway seeds
salt and pepper

Place the cabbage in a colander and sprinkle with salt. Stand for 30 minutes then press gently to remove the excess liquid. Mix the remaining ingredients and chill. *Serves 6-8.*

BAROSSA POTATO SALAD

4 large potatoes, diced
8 rashers bacon, diced
6 shallots, chopped
2 dill chopped cucumbers
2 tablespoons chopped capers
2 hard boiled eggs, chopped
1 cup sour cream
salt
pepper

Place the potatoes in boiling water and cook for 7-10 minutes. Drain and cool. Lightly fry the bacon, drain on kitchen paper. Combine all the ingredients and chill well. Serve in a bowl lined with lettuce. *Serves 6-8.*

CARROT SALAD

4 carrots
¼ cup shredded coconut
2 tablespoons sultanas
½ cup fresh orange juice
2 teaspoons French dressing

Wash and finely grate the raw carrots. Combine with all the remaining ingredients. Chill and serve. *Serves 4.*

SUMMER SALAD

1 lettuce, any variety
4-6 spinach leaves
4 shallots, chopped
1 red capsicum, diced
1 punnet cherry tomatoes
1 avocado, sliced
1 tablespoon sunflower seeds
½ cup walnut pieces

Dressing

2 tablespoons white wine vinegar
3 tablespoons safflower oil
1 tablespoon walnut oil
1 teaspoon raw sugar
salt and pepper

Wash and dry the lettuce, spinach leaves and tomatoes. Combine all the ingredients in a large salad bowl. Blend dressing ingredients, then toss with the dressing and serve immediately. Chopped crisp, fried bacon pieces may be added if desired. *Serves 4.*

SAUCES

JACKAROO SAUCE

2 hot red chillies, seeded and cut into segments
2 cups canned whole tomatoes
2 onions, chopped
1 garlic clove
1 teaspoon ground coriander
½ teaspoon sugar
½ teaspoon salt
2 tablespoons wine vinegar
1 tablespoon chopped parsley

Combine the chillies, tomatoes, onions, garlic, coriander and sugar in an electric blender and blend until smooth. Add salt, vinegar and parsley.

HERB SAUCE

300ml (10 fl oz) carton plain yoghurt, chilled
¼ cup mayonnaise
½ teaspoon dill
½ teaspoon dried chervil
½ teaspoon parsley flakes
½ teaspoon chives
¼ teaspoon salt
¼ teaspoon black pepper
2 hard cooked eggs, chopped

Combine yoghurt, mayonnaise and seasonings. Blend well. Stir in chopped egg.

APPLE SAUCE

450g (15oz) Granny Smith (green) apples
150ml (5 fl oz) water
1 tablespoon sugar
15g (½oz) butter

Peel, core and thinly slice the apples. Put into a pan with the water, sugar and butter or margarine. Cook gently until soft. Beat with a wooden spoon until smooth.

TARTARE SAUCE

1 cup mayonnaise
2 tablespoons chopped gherkin or dill pickle
1½ tablespoons capers, chopped
1 tablespoon chopped chives
¼ teaspoon chervil

Combine all the ingredients and place in an airtight container. Chill and use when required.

VELOUTE SAUCE

2 tablespoons butter
4 tablespoons flour
1½ cups chicken stock
1 egg yolk
1 teaspoon lemon juice
¼ teaspoon salt
freshly ground black pepper

Melt the butter and stir in the flour. Cook over low heat for one minute. Add chicken stock gradually, stirring with a whisk. Simmer for 1 minute until the sauce has thickened. Add egg yolk, lemon juice, salt and pepper.

PARSLEY BUTTER

125g (4oz) butter
½ cup chopped parsley
1 tablespoon lemon juice

Soften the butter and beat in the parsley and juice. Shape into a 2cm cylinder and chill. Cut into slices to serve on grilled meat or fish.

MINT SAUCE

2 tablespoons mint leaves
2 teaspoons sugar
½ tablespoon hot water
2 tablespoons vinegar

Wash and dry the mint leaves. Place on a chopping board with 1 teaspoon sugar. Chop until fine. Put into a sauceboat. Add the rest of the sugar. Stir in the hot water and leave for a few minutes to dissolve sugar. Add the vinegar.

WHITE SAUCE

30g (1oz) butter or margarine
30g (1oz) flour
600ml (1pt) milk
seasoning

Heat the butter gently. Remove from the heat and stir in the flour. Return to the heat and cook gently for a few minutes so that the butter and flour mixture does not brown. Remove the pan from the heat and gradually blend in the cold milk. Bring to the boil and cook, stirring with a wooden spoon, until smooth. Add seasoning.

HOLLANDAISE SAUCE

¾ cup butter
3 egg yolks
½ teaspoon salt
pinch cayenne pepper
juice of 1 lemon

Reserve 2 tablespoons cold butter and heat remaining butter in a small saucepan until hot, but not boiling. Combine in a small saucepan, the egg yolks, salt, pepper and the juice of half a lemon. Place pan over gentle heat. Add 1 tablespoon cold reserved butter and stir constantly until the butter has melted. Add remaining tablespoon of cold butter and continue stirring until melted. Remove the pan from the heat and stir in hot butter gradually. Continue stirring until a thick sauce has formed. Add remaining lemon juice to taste.

CLASSIC BROWN SAUCE

2 cups brown stock
⅔ cup dry red wine
3 tablespoons butter
3 tablespoons flour
2 teaspoons tomato paste

Place the stock and wine in a saucepan and boil until reduced to 1½ cups. In another heavy saucepan, melt the butter and add the flour. Stir with a whisk and cook for 4 minutes or until the flour is light brown. Add the wine mixture gradually, beating with a whisk. Return the sauce to the simmer and cook until thick. Beat in the tomato paste.

SWEET 'N' SOUR SAUCE

2 tablespoons vinegar
1½ tablespoons sugar
1 tablespoon tomato puree
2 tablespoons cornflour
1½ teaspoons soy sauce
300ml (10 fl oz) water
salt
2 teaspoons oil
100g (3oz) chopped, canned pineapple
60g (2oz) very finely chopped onions

▶

Blend vinegar, sugar, tomato puree, cornflour, soy sauce with the water. Put into a saucepan and cook until thick. Add the salt and oil and continue cooking for a few minutes, then stir in pineapple.

MAYONNAISE

4 large egg yolks
½ teaspoon salt
1 teaspoon mild mustard
juice of 1 lemon
2 cups salad oil

Place the egg yolks, salt and mustard in an electric mixer bowl. Beat until the yolks are thick. Add the strained juice of ½ lemon. Beat at top speed until very thick. Add ¼ cup of oil drop by drop. Continue adding the oil very slowly until 1 cup of oil has been used. Add remaining lemon juice and 1 tablespoon of hot water if the mayonnaise is too thick to beat. Add the remaining oil gradually.

TOMATO SAUCE

1kg (2½lb) ripe tomatoes
1 onion

8 cloves
3 tablespoons oil
3 tablespoons flour
salt
freshly ground black pepper

Wash and roughly chop the tomatoes and onion. Heat the oil, then add the flour and cook until smooth and brown, stirring constantly. Add the tomatoes, onion and spices, Cook slowly for 1 hour. Pass through a sieve and use with meat, poulty or vegetables.

HORSERADISH SAUCE

3 tablespoons grated fresh horseradish
1 teaspoon sugar
2 teaspoons powdered English mustard
salt and pepper
wine vinegar
125ml (4 fl oz) thickened cream

Combine all the ingredients except the cream. Use just enough vinegar to mix to a smooth paste. Lightly whip the cream and stir in. Store in a sealed bottle in the refrigerator. Serve with roast beef or steak.

DESSERTS

PAVLOVA

7 egg whites
400g (13oz) castor sugar
1 teaspoon vanilla essence
1 teaspoon vinegar
2 teaspoons cornflour
½ teaspoon cream of tartar

Filling
450ml (15 fl oz) cream, whipped
1 punnet strawberries
3 passionfruit

Beat the egg whites until stiff but not dry. Beat in the castor sugar, teaspoon by teaspoon, adding vanilla, vinegar, cornflour and cream of tartar last. Butter and flour a serving plate. Pipe the mixture onto it and bake in a slow oven 150°C (300°F) for 2 hours, or until cooked. Switch off heat and leave in the oven. When cool, fill with whipped cream. Top with strawberries and passionfruit pulp.

PAVLOVA ROULADE

4 large egg whites
¾ cup castor sugar
¾ cup whipped cream
2 tablespoons passionfruit pulp
1 cup strawberries, sliced

Grease and line a Swiss roll tin. Preheat the oven to 180°C (350°F). Beat the egg whites until stiff; gradually add the sugar. Beat until smooth and glossy. Spread the meringue into the Swiss roll tin and bake for 8-10 minutes, then turn onto a sheet of greaseproof paper. Remove the paper and set aside for 10 minutes. Spread with the cream, passionfruit pulp and sliced strawberries. Roll firmly and chill. Serve with extra cream.

LEMON SYLLABUB

500ml (1pt) double cream
(unpasteurised if possible)
grated rind and juice of 2 lemons
½ cup (4 fl oz) sherry
1 cup (8oz) castor sugar

Beat the cream, sugar, lemon rind and juice until stiff. Add the sherry, mix thoroughly. Place in serving dishes and chill for 3-4 hours. Serve with macerated fresh fruits or glace fruit.

MARY REIBY'S PORT WINE JELLY

4½ tablespoons gelatine
200ml (7½ fl oz) water
6 tablespoons sugar
3 tablespoons lemon juice
200ml (7½ fl oz) tawny port

Soak the gelatine in the water and stand the container in hot water to dissolve. When dissolved, add the sugar, strained lemon juice and port. Pour into a jelly mould and refrigerate for 4-6 hours. Serve in tall glasses with whipped cream.

LIME JELLY

1½ teaspoons gelatine
dissolved in 80ml (3 fl oz) cold water
400ml (13 fl oz) boiling water
180g (6oz) sugar
150g (5oz) lime juice
1½ teaspoons grated lemon rind

Dissolve the gelatine in cold water, add the sugar and stand the bowl over boiling water bath. Cool a little. Add the lime juice and lemon rind, mix and pour into a wet mould. Chill until firm. Unmould onto a cold plate and surround with peeled, sliced kiwi fruit and bananas.

CHOCOLATE MOUSSE

120g (4oz) dark chocolate
4 eggs

Melt chocolate over hot water. Separate yolks from whites and add yolks to chocolate one at a time, combine well. Beat the egg whites until almost stiff and gently fold through the chocolate mixture. Pour into individual serving dishes and allow to set overnight. Serve with a swirl of whipped cream.

PEACH MELBA

6 ripe, freestone peaches
2 cups sauterne
1 cup water
¾ cup sugar
vanilla ice cream

▶

To prepare the peaches, bring a pan of water to the boil and blanch the peaches for 30-50 seconds. Remove from the water and gently rub the skin off with a towel. Slice the peaches, combine the wine, water and sugar, then bring to the boil and simmer for 5 minutes. Add the sliced peaches and poach for 5-7 minutes – do not overcook! Allow to cool in the syrup. To assemble the dessert, place a few peaches in a long stem parfait glass, add a scoop of ice cream and another layer of peaches. Top with the raspberry sauce and serve accompanied with a vanilla wafer.

Melba Sauce
500g (1lb) frozen or fresh raspberries
¼ cup icing sugar mixture
2 tablespoons kirsch
vanilla wafer

Combine the raspberries, sugar and kirsch, and let stand for ½ hour. Puree in a blender and strain to remove the seeds.

FLUMMERY

1 tablespoon flour
1 cup hot water
1½ tablespoons gelatine
¼ cup cold water
¾ cup sugar
1 cup orange juice
juice of 1 lemon
1 tablespoon passionfruit pulp

Mix the flour to a paste with a little cold water. Add the hot water and stir well. Bring to the boil and simmer for 1 minute. Combine the cold water, gelatine, fruit juices, sugar and passionfruit. Stir into the flour mixture and return to the boil. Remove from the heat, pour into a mixing bowl and cool. Beat with an electric mixer until light and fluffy. Pour into a serving bowl and refrigerate overnight. Serve decorated with whipped cream and extra passionfruit.

VANILLA ICE CREAM

2 eggs
2 egg yolks
½ cup sugar
1 vanilla bean
1¼ cups milk
1¼ cups thickened cream, lightly whipped

Beat the eggs and egg yolks with the sugar until pale yellow and creamy. Put the vanilla bean into the milk and heat gently. Stand for 10 minutes. Strain the milk onto the egg mixture and place in the top half of a double boiler and cook the custard until it coats the back of a metal spoon. Cool. Fold in the cream. Pour into a container and freeze.

PASSIONFRUIT ICE

2 cups hot water
1 teaspoon gelatine
½ cup skim milk powder
1 teaspoon vinegar
4 passionfruit
1 egg white
1 tablespoon lemon juice
liquid sweetener

Dissolve gelatine in hot water, add skim milk powder. Beat well. Pour into freezing tray, freeze until set. Spoon ice into mixing bowl, add vinegar, lemon juice and egg white. Beat until very light and smooth, 10 to 15 minutes on electric mixer. Stir in passionfruit pulp and liquid sweetener. Pour into container or freezing tray. Cover and freeze until firm.

LEMON PASSIONFRUIT PIE

1 tin condensed milk
3 passionfruit
1 sweet rich shortcrust pastry case
1 lemon

Mix tin of condensed milk with pulp of passionfruit and juice of one large lemon, mix well, and place in pie case. Cover with whipped cream and chill.

JILLEROO'S PANCAKES

1 cup flour
pinch salt
1 egg, beaten
1¼ cups milk

Sift the flour and salt into a bowl, make a well in the centre and gradually stir in the egg and milk. Beat quickly to remove any lumps. Pour a small amount of the batter into a hot greased pan. When the mixture is set turn and cook for 20-30 seconds. Repeat until all the batter is cooked. This mixture makes 8-10 pancakes. Serve with golden syrup and clotted cream or fresh strawberries.

GRANNY'S WINE TRIFLE

2 sponge sandwiches
plum jam
1½ cups sweet or cream sherry
1 litre (32 fl oz) thick, stirred custard
400g (13oz) grated, dark cooking chocolate
300ml (10 fl oz) whipped cream
3 passionfruit or strawberries

Cut the sponge into pieces that will fit a large glass bowl. Spread the sponge pieces generously with plum jam. Place a layer of sponge in the bowl. Soak with sherry. Pour a layer of custard over and sprinkle thickly with chocolate. Repeat layers finishing with custard and chocolate. Cover with whipped cream. Decorate with fruit. Allow to stand for 4-6 hours in refrigerator before serving.

STRAWBERRY STUPENDA

300g (10oz) strawberries
150g (5oz) sugar
1 tablespoon lemon juice
1½ tablespoons gelatine
2 tablespoons water
1 egg white
300ml (10 fl oz) cream

Wash and hull strawberries (keep a few for decorating) and sprinkle with sugar. Put strawberries in a saucepan and slowly bring to the boil to soften the fruit. Add sugar and lemon juice, and stir over low heat until the sugar dissolves. Soak the gelatine in water and then dissolve in hot strawberry liquid. Beat puree with whisk or beater to break up the fruit and make it fairly smooth. Allow to cool. Lightly beat egg white and brush the inside of mould with part of it. Beat remainder of egg white with chilled cream until thick. Fold cream gently into cooled strawberry puree. Pour into mould then chill until set. Carefully unmould and decorate with sugared strawberries.

APPLE FOOL

450g (15oz) Granny Smith (green) apples
150g (5oz) sugar
4 tablespoons lemon juice
2 tablespoons finely chopped lemon peel
200ml (7 fl oz) water
200ml (7 fl oz) cream, whipped

Peel, core and chop the apples. Add sugar, lemon juice, lemon peel and water. Cook until soft then put through a wire sieve. Cool and refrigerate. When cold, fold in the whipped cream and pile into a serving dish. Serve very cold. *Serves 6-8.*

FLOATING ISLANDS

4 egg whites
½ cup castor sugar
3 cups milk
6 tablespoons sugar
2 tablespoons flour
2 egg yolks, beaten
1 teaspoon vanilla essence

Beat the egg whites to soft peaks then gradually add the ½ cup sugar and continue beating until very stiff. In a large, shallow pan heat the milk and remaining sugar. Bring to simmering point, stirring occasionally. Place heaped spoonsful of the meringue mixture into the hot milk and poach for 1-2 minutes on each side. Remove with a slotted spoon and drain on paper towels. Mix ¼ cup of the hot milk with the flour and stir until the mixture is smooth. Beat in the egg yolks and combine with the remaining hot milk. Bring to the boil stirring constantly. Cook for 2 minutes, remove from the heat and add the vanilla. Pour the custard into a glass serving bowl and drop the floating islands on the top. Chill and serve.

GRAMMA PIE

250g (8oz) sweet short crust pastry
1½ cups gramma or pumpkin, cooked and mashed
3 eggs
¾ cup brown sugar
½ cup milk
½ cup cream
grated rind and juice of 1 lemon
½ teaspoon nutmeg
½ teaspoon ground ginger
⅛ teaspoon ground cloves
2 tablespoons sweet sherry

Roll out the pastry and line a 23cm (10in) pie plate. Trim the pastry and cut another 25mm (1in) strip. Place around the edge of the pastry so that there is a double crust. Crimp and chill. Mix together the gramma and the remaining ingredients. Spoon the mixture into the pastry and bake in a hot oven 200°C (400°F) for 15 minutes, then reduce the heat to 180°C (350°F) for another 35-40 minutes. Serve warm.

COBBER'S CRUMBLE

1kg (2lb) stewed fruit – apple, rhubarb, peaches etc.
1 cup coarse biscuit crumbs
2 tablespoons wholemeal flour
2 tablespoons soft brown sugar
60g (2oz) butter, melted
1 teaspoon cinnamon

Arrange the fruit in an ovenproof dish. Combine all the dry ingredients and add the melted butter. The mixture should resemble coarse breadcrumbs. Spread evenly over the fruit. Top with a little extra brown sugar. Bake in a hot oven 200°C (400°F) for 20-25 minutes. Serve with stirred custard or fresh cream.

Stirred Custard
2 eggs
2 egg yolks
⅓ cup sugar
500ml (1pt) milk
vanilla pod

Beat the eggs, yolks and sugar until pale yellow. Slowly heat the milk with vanilla pod and stand for 10 minutes. Remove the pod. Pour the milk onto the egg mixture and place in the top of a double boiler. Cook until the mixture thickens, stirring constantly. Serve hot or cold.

APPLE AND QUINCE PIE

750g (1½lb) Granny Smith (green) apples
250g (½lb) quinces, peeled and sliced
125ml (¼pt) water
1 tablespoon grated lemon rind
2 whole cloves
sugar to taste
egg white
250g (½lb) rich short crust pastry

Peel, core and quarter the apples. Place the peels and cores in a saucepan and cover with the water. Simmer for 30 minutes. Strain and cool. Pile the apples and quince into a deep pie dish. Add the lemon rind, cloves and sugar to taste. Pour the strained liquid onto the fruit. Cover the pie with the pastry. Glaze the top with a little beaten egg white and sprinkle with castor sugar. Make a slash in the top of the pie to allow steam to escape. Bake at 200°C (400°F) for 15 minutes then reduce to 180°C (350°F) for 35 minutes. Serve hot with fresh cream.

JANE BARKER'S STEAMED DATE PUDDING

500g (½lb) pitted dates
250g (¼lb) suet
3 cups fresh breadcrumbs
¾ cup castor sugar
1 egg, beaten
½ cup milk
4 tablespoons flour
2 teaspoons baking powder

Finely chop the dates and suet. Mix the breadcrumbs and suet together, add the remaining ingredients and mix thoroughly. Fill a greased pudding basin, cover tightly and steam for 2½-3 hours. Serve with stirred custard or fresh cream.

COUSIN KATE'S PUDDING

1 egg
30g (1oz) butter
1 cup flour
½ cup sugar
vanilla essence

Cream butter and sugar, add beaten egg. Fold in flour and enough milk to moisten, not too thin. Pour into casserole dish and bake 20 minutes to ½ hour. Take from oven and while hot cover with jam and serve with custard or cream.

GRANDMAMA'S CHRISTMAS PUDDING

2½ cups flour
1 cup soft brown sugar
1 teaspoon bicarbonate of soda
1½ cups white breadcrumbs
2 teaspoons mixed spice
3 cups mixed dried fruit
1 tablespoon mixed peel
2 teaspoons grated orange rind
180g (6oz) grated suet
3 eggs, beaten
½ cup brandy

Mix together the dry ingredients. Add the fruits and rind. Combine the suet, eggs and brandy and pour into the fruit mixture and stir thoroughly. Pour the mixture into a prepared cloth. Tie securely and cover with boiling water. Cook for 4 hours. Put in cool, dry place until Christmas. On Christmas day, cook for 1-1½ hours before serving. To prepare a pudding cloth: plunge a 75cm (2½ft) square of cheesecloth or calico into boiling water. Wring out and dust with flour. *Serves 6.*

CAKES & BISCUITS

AUSSIE SPONGE SANDWICH

3 eggs
¾ cup castor sugar
1 cup self raising flour
pinch salt
1 teaspoon butter, melted
3 tablespoons hot water

Grease 2 x 18cm (7in) sandwich tins and dust lightly with a little flour. Set oven temperature at moderate 180°C (350°F). Separate the eggs. Beat the whites until stiff. Add sugar gradually, whisking until thick. Add the yolks, all at the one time, and whisk until thoroughly combined. Sift the flour and salt together twice. Now sift the flour once more into the egg mixture, folding it in lightly and evenly. Fold in the melted butter and hot water quickly and lightly. Pour into the prepared sandwich tins and bake in a preheated moderate 180°C (350°F) oven for 20 minutes. Turn out and cool on a wire rack. When cold fill with raspberry jam or passionfruit and whipped cream.

RIVERLAND ORANGE CAKE

125g (4oz) butter or margarine
½ cup castor sugar
1 teaspoon grated orange rind
1 egg, beaten
2 cups self raising flour
pinch salt
⅔ cup skim milk

Cream margarine, sugar and orange rind. Add egg, beat well. Fold in flour and salt, alternately with milk. Place into a greased and lined 28cm x 18cm (11in x 7in) lamington tin. Bake in a moderately low oven 180°C (350°F) for 30-35 minutes.

BLAKEHURST SPONGE

4 eggs
120g (4oz) plain flour
180g (6oz) castor sugar
½ lemon juice and rind
pinch of salt

Beat egg whites, add castor sugar gradually, beating well after each addition. Add egg yolks one at a time. Beat well. Fold in lemon and rind. Fold in flour and salt after sifting 3 times. Pour into one 20cm (8in) cake tin or two tins greased and powdered with ½ flour and ½ icing sugar. Bake 20 minutes at 200°C (400°F) in oven.

LEMON CHIFFON CHEESECAKE

Crumb Crust Base
1½ cups plain sweet biscuit crumbs
90g (3oz) butter
½ teaspoon cinnamon
½ teaspoon nutmeg

Lemon Chiffon Filling
1½ tablespoons gelatine
½ cup cold water
250g (½lb) cream cheese
1 x 300g (10oz) carton plain yoghurt
3 egg yolks
¾ cup sugar
pinch salt
2 teaspoons grated lemon rind
1 tablespoon lemon juice
3 egg whites
½ cup castor sugar
150ml (5 fl oz) cream, whipped

Melt butter, remove from heat. Stir in biscuit crumbs and spices. Press firmly onto base only of a greased 20cm (8in) springform tin. Bake in a moderate oven 180°C (350°F) for about 8 minutes. Allow to cool thoroughly before using. Soften gelatine in the cold water. Sieve the cream cheese and beat with the yoghurt until smooth. In the top of a double saucepan beat egg yolks with the sugar and salt. Cook over hot water until thick and creamy. Add softened gelatine and stir until dissolved. Cool slightly and stir in lemon rind and juice. Add the yoghurt cream cheese mixture. Beat egg whites until stiff. Add sugar gradually and beat until sugar is dissolved. Gently fold the gelatine mixture through the meringue. Finally, fold in the whipped cream. Pour over cold crumb crust and chill for 24 hours. Remove springform ring 20 minutes before serving.

LAMINGTONS

125g (4oz) butter
180g (5oz) self raising flour
½ cup milk
2 eggs
125g (4oz) sugar
½ teaspoon vanilla
2 teaspoons flour

Cream the butter, add the sifted flour and beat for 1 minute. Beat the eggs and beat in the sugar, then gradually fold into the creamed butter and flour. Stir in the milk. Lastly, fold in the extra flour. Pour into a greased slab tin and bake at 160°C (325°F) for 25 minutes.

Icing
500g (½lb) sifted icing sugar
2 egg whites
4 tablespoons grated chocolate
125g (4oz) butter
2 teaspoons sherry
dessicated coconut

Dissolve the chocolate over hot water. Mix the butter and icing sugar. Add the chocolate and sherry and mix to a stiff paste. Beat the egg whites until stiff and fold into the icing. Cut the cake into 5cm (2in) squares. Coat with the icing and dredge in the coconut.

ROCK CAKES

2 cups self raising flour
180g (6oz) butter or margarine
½ cup castor sugar
2 tablespoons sultanas
1 x 50g (2oz) egg, beaten
1 tablespoon skim milk

Sift flour, rub in margarine. Add sugar and fruits. Add egg and milk to dry ingredients and mix well. Place heaped tablespoonsful of mixture onto greased scone slides. Bake in a hot oven 200°C (400°F) for 15-20 minutes.

BASIC BUTTER CAKE

125g (4oz) butter
1 teaspoon vanilla
¾ cup castor sugar
2 eggs
2 cups self raising flour
pinch salt
½ cup milk

Set oven at moderate temperature 180°C (350°F). Prepare 2 x 20cm (8in) sandwich tins by brushing with melted butter or oil, lining base with greased greaseproof paper and dusting lightly with flour. In a large bowl cream butter with vanilla, using a wooden spoon, until softened. Add sugar gradually, beating until mixture is light and fluffy. Lightly beat eggs and beat in gradually to prevent curdling. If using an electric mixer, add 1 teaspoon of milk while beating butter and sugar. (This will help to dissolve sugar crystals.) Add eggs one at a time and beat well after each. Sift flour and salt three times onto a sheet of greaseproof paper. Using a large metal spoon, fold lightly into creamed mixture in three lots, alternating with milk, until mixture is smooth and all flour incorporated. Drop into prepared tins. Lightly smooth top and bake in a moderate oven 180°C (350°F) for 25-35 minutes. Turn out and cool on wire rack.

BOILED FRUIT CAKE

2½ cups mixed fruit
1 cup granulated sugar
mixed spice
teaspoon butter or margarine
½ cup water
4½ cups sifted plain flour
2 well beaten eggs

Boil the ingredients for 10 minutes, mixing well. Let it cool. Add flour and eggs. Blend very well. Put the mixture into a greased and lined 20cm (8in) cake tin and bake in a slow oven 120°C (250°F) for about 2 hours.

MATILDA'S DATE LOAF

1½ cups plain flour
3 teaspoons baking powder
¼ teaspoon salt
60g (2oz) butter
¾ cup brown sugar
1 egg
1 cup dates, chopped
¼ cup walnuts, chopped
1 teaspoon bicarbonate of soda
1 cup boiling water

Sift the flour, baking powder and salt into a bowl. Melt the butter; add the brown sugar, egg, dates and walnuts and mix well. Fold the flour through the mixture, and lastly add the bicarbonate of soda and boiling water. Mix well. Pour into a greased and lined loaf tin. Bake in a moderate oven 180°C (350°F) for 40-45 minutes or until cooked.

PUMPKIN SPICE CAKE

125g (¼lb) butter
2 teaspoons orange rind
¾ cup castor sugar
1 cup cooked mashed pumpkin
2 eggs
1 cup sultanas
2 cups self raising flour
½ teaspoon each of ginger,
mixed spice and cinnamon
½ cup milk

Cream the butter, sugar and rind until light, add the pumpkin and beat for 2 minutes. Beat in the eggs and fruit and lastly fold in the sifted flour and spices alternately with the milk. Bake in a greased 20cm (8in) ring tin at 190°C (375°F) for 40-50 minutes. Cool on a rack and dust with icing sugar.

CUSTARD TART

180g (6oz) biscuit pastry
egg, white only
raspberry jam

Custard
3 eggs
2 tablespoons sugar
1½ tablespoons cornflour
400ml (13 fl oz) heated milk
vanilla essence

Line 25cm (10in) pie plate, taking care not to have any thin or broken pastry. Take a little white of egg, reserved from eggs in custard, and glaze surface of pastry very lightly. Allow this to dry before filling shell. Spread thinly with raspberry jam. Beat eggs, sugar and cornflour till creamy. Add warm milk and vanilla essence and mix well. Spoon custard gently into shell and sprinkle with nutmeg. Bake in moderate oven 180°C (350°F) for about 30 minutes, or until set.

GINGERBREAD

250g (½lb) flour
1 teaspoon powdered ginger
½ teaspoon cinnamon
60g (2oz) butter
1 egg
½ teaspoon bicarbonate of soda
2 tablespoons golden syrup
2 tablespoons hot water
60g (2oz) brown sugar

Sift the flour and spices into a bowl. Rub in the butter. Lightly beat the egg and mix with the warmed syrup, sugar and hot water. Stir all the ingredients thoroughly, pour into a slab tin and bake for 20 minutes at 190°C (375°F).

DAMPER

250g (½lb) plain flour
1 teaspoon baking powder
1 teaspoon bicarbonate of soda
2 teaspoons butter
150ml (5 fl oz) milk
pinch salt

Melt butter in the milk, and beat well. Add flour and mix into dough. Turn onto floured tray and sprinkle top with flour after mixture has been shaped. Cook in a moderately hot oven 190°C (375°F) until brown.

CELERY AND SESAME MUFFINS

1½ cups self raising flour
½ teaspoon salt
3 tablespoons butter
½ cup chopped onion
1 cup grated cheese
1 egg, well beaten
½ cup milk
1 tablespoon sesame seeds
1 tablespoon celery seeds

Sift flour and salt into a basin. Heat 2 tablespoons of the butter. Add onion and cook until soft. Cool. To sifted ingredients add half cheese and cooled onion. Mix beaten egg and milk. Add to dry ingredients. Mix to a soft dough. Two thirds fill greased deep patty tins with the mixture. Sprinkle tops with remaining cheese, sesame and celery seeds. Melt remaining butter and drizzle over the top. Bake in a hot oven 200°C (400°F) for 15-20 minutes. Serve with butter.

COACH HOUSE PIKELETS

1 cup self raising flour, sifted
pinch salt
1 tablespoon sugar

1 egg, lightly beaten
½ cup buttermilk
1 tablespoon melted butter

Place the dry ingredients in a bowl. Mix the egg, milk and butter together and stir into the flour mixture. Mix to a smooth butter. Heat a fry pan or flat griddle, and drop spoonsful of the batter onto the pan. When the mixture bubbles on the top, turn. Serve with strawberry jam and whipped cream.

PLAIN SCONES

2 cups self raising flour
½ teaspoon salt
1½ tablespoons butter
¾ cup milk

Sift flour and salt into a basin. Rub butter in lightly, using tips of fingers. Add milk all at once, reserving a little for glazing. Mix quickly to a soft dough – use extra milk if necessary. Turn dough on to floured surface, knead lightly and quickly. Roll out about 1cm (½in) thick. Cut out with floured knife or round cutter. Glaze with milk and place fairly close together on greased slide. Bake in a very hot oven 230°C (450°F) for 10-12 minutes.

PIONEER PUMPKIN SCONES

½ cup sugar
3 tablespoons butter
1 egg
2 cups cold pureed pumpkin (any variety)
3 cups plain flour
6 teaspoons baking powder

Lightly grease an oven or biscuit slide. Cream the butter and sugar. Add the egg and pumpkin and beat. Stir in the sifted, dry ingredients to form a soft dough. Turn onto a lightly floured board and pat down or roll to 2cm (¾in) thickness. Cut into rounds with a 5cm (2in) biscuit cutter. Place close together on the prepared slide. Brush the tops with a little milk. Bake in a hot oven 200°C (400°F) for 10-15 minutes. Serve hot with butter and golden syrup or honey.

ANZAC BISCUITS

180g (6oz) rolled oats
180g (6oz) plain flour
180g (6oz) desiccated coconut
180g (6oz) sugar
1½ teaspoons baking powder
200g (7oz) butter
2 tablespoons golden syrup

Mix all the dry ingredients together in a bowl. Melt the butter. Pour over the flour mixture and add the syrup. Shape into small balls. Flatten them with a fork onto a buttered baking sheet and bake in a medium-low oven 140°C (300°F) for 15 minutes.

AUSSIE GEMS

1 tablespoon butter
2 tablespoons sugar
1½ cups plain flour
1 egg
½ cup milk

Cream butter and sugar, add egg. Then add sifted flour alternately with milk. Put into hot greased gem irons. Bake in a very hot oven 230°C (450°F) for 15 minutes. Serve like scones.

SWEET SHORT CRUST PASTRY

250g (8oz) plain flour
125g (4oz) butter or margarine
⅓ cup castor sugar
1 egg yolk
squeeze of lemon juice ▶

Sieve the flour into a bowl. Rub in the shortening with finger tips until the mixture resembles fine bread-crumbs. Add the sugar. Mix the egg yolk and lemon juice and stir into the mixture with a knife. Draw the dough together to form a ball. Knead gently on a floured board and chill. Use as required. For savoury pies delete the sugar and add a pinch of salt.

BUSHWACKER'S BUSTERS

500g (1lb) self raising flour
1 cup soured milk
golden syrup

In a bowl, mix together the flour and milk and stir quickly with a knife blade. Knead into round balls the size of an egg. Bake in a hot oven 200°C (400°F) or push onto the end of a thick stick and bake in hot ashes. When cooked, remove from the stick and fill the cavity with golden syrup. Eat while hot.

BRANDY SNAPS

60g (2oz) butter
⅓ cup brown sugar
2 tablespoons golden syrup
½ teaspoon lemon juice
½ cup plain flour

1 teaspoon ground ginger
whipped cream flavoured with brandy

Melt the butter. Add the brown sugar, golden syrup and lemon juice. Warm over a low heat. Remove from the heat and stir in the flour and ginger. Place 4 spoonsful of the mixture onto a biscuit slide and bake at 180°C (350°F) for 5-6 minutes. Remove from the oven and stand for 1 minute. Gently remove from the slide with spatula and roll around the handle of a wooden spoon. Cool and fill with whipped cream.

HOT CROSS BUNS

4 cups plain flour
1 teaspoon mixed spice
½ teaspoon ground cinnamon
1 teaspoon salt
60g (2oz) butter
½ cup castor sugar
¾ cup currants or sultanas
¼ cup chopped mixed peel (optional)
30g (1oz) compressed yeast
½ cup lukewarm water
½ cup lukewarm milk
1 egg
slightly beaten egg white

Sift flour, spices and salt. Rub in butter, stir in sugar and fruit. Blend yeast with little water. Add remaining water and milk. Make well in centre of flour. Pour in yeast mixture and egg, adding nearly all at once and make into a soft dough. Knead in basin or on floured board until smooth and elastic. Place in a greased covered basin. Leave in a warm place until doubled in bulk. Pat dough to 1½cm (½-¾in) thickness. Cut into 16 even sized pieces. Knead each round. Place 2½cm (1in) apart on greased baking tray. Cover, allow to rise in warm place for 20-30 minutes. Brush with egg white and bake in hot oven 200°C (400°F) for approximately 15 minutes. For baked on crosses, prepare mixture of 4 tablespoons self raising flour and 2 teaspoons cold water. Beat until smooth. Fill into forcing bag. Pipe crosses of flour mixture before baking. When cooked, brush with glaze.

Glaze
2 tablespoons water
¼ teaspoon gelatine dissolved over low heat

Add 1 teaspoon sugar and stir until dissolved and thickened. Brush over buns whilst hot.

WATTLE PIKELETS

1 cup plain flour
1 egg
½ cup milk
2 teaspoons baking powder
1 tablespoon honey
2 cups opened, washed wattle flowers

Sift the flour and baking powder into a bowl and make a well in the centre. Lightly beat the egg and milk together. Mix with the dry ingredients, honey and egg mixture, and stir until smooth. Place tablespoonsful of the mixture onto a flat pan. Cook until tiny bubbles appear on the surface and turn. Serve with honey or golden syrup and whipped cream.

BUTTERNUT SNAPS

125g (4oz) butter
1 cup sugar
1 egg
1 cup coconut
½ teaspoon vanilla
2 tablespoons golden syrup
1½ cups self raising flour

Cream butter and sugar until light and fluffy. Add egg, and beat well. Mix in coconut, vanilla, golden syrup and sifted flour and blend well. Roll heaped teaspoons of mixture into small balls. Place on lightly greased oven trays. Press down with fork. Bake in moderate oven 180°C (350°F) for 20-25 minutes.

HERBS & SPICES

HERBS

The general heading "Herbs" denotes a large number of aromatic plants used in cooking.

DRIED HERBS   Herbs should be harvested just before the buds open into full flower for the greatest flavour and abundance of natural oils. Gather them in dry weather, hang them up to dry in bundles in an airy room, or lay them on paper in a dark cupboard. Oven-drying is not as successful as some of the flavour is lost. The drying time varies from about twelve days to three weeks. When dry, strip the leaves from the stalks on to paper and place them into clean, dry, air-tight jars which have been labelled.

ANGELICA   Angelica grows to 2 metres in height. Candied angelica is made from the stalk and leaf stems. Oil, distilled from the seeds and roots is used in flavouring liqueurs and wines, and the leaves are used in flavouring stewed fruit.

BALM   Balm, or lemon balm as it is frequently called, can be added to salads, mushroom dishes and sweet jellies. The crushed leaves give off a pleasant lemon scent, and a few, added to a teapot with tea leaves, will produce a refreshing drink. Balm is an important ingredient in pot pourri, where its tang helps to offset the sweetness of the flower scents.

BASIL   There are more than 40 varieties of this sharp, piquant herb, but the best known are the sweet and bush basil. Sweet basil is particularly suitable for drying and therefore the easiest to obtain in the dried form. Basil adds interest to tomatoes, pasta dishes, rice, liver, kidneys and fish.

BAY LEAVES   The bay tree is a member of the laurel family. Bay leaves are always an ingredient of bouquet garni; they can also be used in soups, stews, stock, fish, eat, sauces and poultry. Bay leaves may be used straight from the tree or dried.

CHERVIL   Chervil has a serrated and fernlike leaf, with a flavour reminiscent of aniseed. Use dried chervil with discretion in soups, stews, sauces, gravies and with fish and meat. Fresh leaves can be chopped and sprinkled fairly liberally on salads and vegetables.

CHIVES   Chives stem from a small bulb and belong to the lily family. The thin grass-like leaves are believed to stimulate the appetite, and have a mild onion flavour. Chopped chives can be used in cream cheese, mashed potato, scrambled egg.

GARLIC   Garlic is the bulb of a plant belonging to the lily family. In appearance it resembles an irregular shaped onion. This is composed of several "cloves" or segments, each one encasesd in flaky, white skin.

MARJORAM   There are many varieties of marjoram. Sweet marjoram is the type most widely used in cooking. The plant grows to about 1 metre in height and its grey-green leaves have a spicy, mint flavour. This herb may be used in bouquet garni, beef, pork, lamb, cheese and fish dishes, also soups and sauces.

MINT Fresh mint can usually be bought, it is easy to grow in the home garden. There are many varieties of mint, the best known is the curly-leaved spearmint. Applemint which smells strongly of apples is ideal for mint sauce. Cook several sprigs of fresh mint or a teaspoon of dried mint, with vegetables, especially peas and net potatoes. Serve some in iced tea and summer fruit drinks. Mint sauce or mint jelly is the traditional accompaniment to roast lamb.

OREGANO Oregano, the wild marjoram of Italy and Spain is prominent in the cooking of these two countries. The name **Origanum** comes from the Greek words meaning "joy of the mountains". Oregano has a strong, pungent flavour and is one of the ingredients in chilli powder. This herb gives a piquant flavour to such dishes as pizza and chilli con carne, and combines well with tomatoes.

PARSLEY One of the most widely used and versatile of all herbs, parsley is rich in vitamin C and also contains iron, calcium and vitamin A. There are many varieties of parsley being, fern-leaved parsley, curled parsley and "Italian" parsley. Unlike other herbs, which should be used with discretion, a liberal amount of chopped parsley can be added to many kinds of dishes. Use fresh or dried sprigs as a garnish; add chopped or dried parsley to soups, stews, egg dishes, dumplings and sauces.

ROSEMARY The variety of rosemary generally cultivated today grows to about 1 metre in height and is a straight-branched bush with grey-green, spiny leaves. It is the leaves that are used in cooking – either fresh or dried and crumbled. The pungent and refreshing scent of the leaves is used in cool drinks, stuffings, garnishes and soups and with lamb and sauteed potatoes.

SAGE There are many varieties of this particular pungent herb. For cooking, the narrow-leaved sage with blue flowers or the broad-leaved sage are perhaps the best. Use as a seasoning for meat loaves, cheese and egg dishes or with fish – and, of course, in sage and onion stuffing. Try rubbing a joint with sage before roasting – but remember its strength so use sparingly.

SAVORY The two best known types of savory are the annual summer and perennial winter varieties – they are similar in flavour – peppery and aromatic, with the elusive scent of rosemary and the pungency of sage. It can be used in omelettes, salads, also with lamb, pork and veal or combined with other herbs in stuffings.

SORREL An acid tasting green leaf used as a flavouring for salads, omelettes and soups. Sorrel may also be prepared in the same way as spinach and served with veal or fish.

TARRAGON There are two accepted culinary types, known as French tarragon and Russian tarragon – but the French with it superior flavour, is used most in cooking. Tarragon is the essential ingredient in bearnaise sauce. Its sharp taste blends with fish and shellfish. Mayonnaise, hollandaise sauce, and French dressing benefit from a pinch of tarragon and fresh and chopped, it is delicious sprinkled over salads.

THYME Of the many varieties of thyme, lemon scented and garden thyme are the best known and most used in the kitchen. Basically the plant is small, bushy, with tiny dark green leaves and purple flowers. A sprig of thyme is one of the bouquet garni ingredients. Use it also to season meats, soups, vegetables, stuffings and foremeat.

HERB COMBINATIONS

BOUQUET GARNI A bunch or "faggot" of herbs, used to flavour stews, casseroles and sauces. Usually consists of fresh sprigs of parsley, thyme, marjoram, rosemary, a bayleaf, peppercorns and cloves tied in muslin. (If unavailable use dried herbs).

FINE HERBS The "fine herbs" in former times was used to signify mixed chopped herbs – parsley, chervil, chives, fennel and tarragon with other aromatic plants. In French, "fine herbs" usually means chopped parsley. The combination of herbs may be used in omelettes, meat, chicken and fish dishes.

MIXED HERBS A blend of popular Australian dried herbs – usually oregano, basil, thyme and rosemary.

SPICES

Spices are produced from a wide range of aromatic plants and trees. Spices may be derived from any part of these plants or trees rich in flavour and aroma, eg roots, stems, bark, buds.

ALLSPICE Allspice (known as Jamaican Pepper) is the dried fruit of the pimento tree – and no relation to the pepper of that name. It is so named because of its resemblance to the combined flavours of nutmeg, cloves and cinnamon. Available whole or ground, allspice is used for pickling, fruit preserving, soups, gravies, cakes, puddings, boiled meats.

CAYENNE Cayenne pepper is made from the ground brilliant red pods of the various species of dried chilli or capsicum. The plant is ornamental, and is grown in many parts of the world. Depending on its country of origin, cayenne varies in pungency, but all types are very hot and should be used with discretion. It is an important ingredient in curry powder.

CHILLI POWDER Originally the spice came from Mexico using a small bright red chilli known as bird's-eye pepper. This made the best and hottest chilli powder. The strength of different powder varies with the brand – from mild to very hot. It can be a mixture of dried chilli peppers, aromatic seeds, spices and herbs. Use to your own personal taste.

CINNAMON The cinnamon tree is an evergreen laurel. The thin bark is peeled from the tree and rolled into sticks as it dries, forming stick cinnamon. True cinnamon grows in Ceylon and India, **Cassia**, a member of the same family comes from South East Asia and is almost identical in flavour. Cinnamon has a mellow, slightly sweet flavour that blends with both sweet and savoury foods. Use ground cinnamon in cakes, milk and fruit puddings. Stick cinnamon use in drinks, pickles, chutneys, stewing fruits.

CLOVES   The name clove is derived from the Latin word **Clavus**, which means nail – it resembles a nail form. Cloves are the buds of an evergreen tree. Used extensively in cookery, they are available whole or ground. Their penetrating aromatic flavour makes careful use essential – 2 or 3 cloves are generally sufficient for most dishes. A traditional use is in apple pie; ground cloves are used in cakes and biscuits.

GINGER   Ginger, the root of the plant, can be obtained in four different forms – green (fresh root); ground (dried and powdered root); preserved (cooked in syrup and tinned or bottled); crystallised (cooked, drained and rolled in sugar). Ginger is an important ingredient in the blending of curry powder. Green ginger (fresh) is used in savoury foods. Ground ginger is used in sweet and savoury recipes.

MACE   Mace, the fleshy covering of nutmeg, with a similar but stronger flavour, is available in "blade" and powdered form. Use it in preserving, flavouring fish, fish sauces and stuffings.

NUTMEG   From the same tree as mace, nutmeg is the kernel of the fruit; available in whole nut or ground form, the nuts should be grated before use. One nutmeg will generally produce 3 teaspoonsful when grated, but, for full flavour, prepare only as much as needed at the time, then store remainder of nut until required again. Although generally used in sweet recipes, nutmeg may be used with meats and poultry.

PAPRIKA   The best paprika is now said to come from Hungary. Paprika is made from the dried, ground pods of a variety of sweet red pepper or capsicum; a cheaper quality is sometimes made from the seed themselves. Has a mild, slightly sweet flavour, and should be a right bright red. Paprika is quite often regarded only as a garnish, but it is a good spice to use for flavouring.

PEPPER   Black and white pepper both come from the berry of a perennial vine. For black pepper – it is the whole peppercorn which is picked, dried; then they become dark in colour, wrinkled and very hot. For white pepper – it is the same berry with the dark outer husk removed, leaving the inner seed, milder in flavour and parchment coloured. Pepper is almost indispensable in savoury cooking. Usually black is preferable, although it is better to use white in pale coloured foods or sauces.

SAFFRON   Saffron is obtained from the orange coloured stigmas of a mauve flowering crocus native to Asia and parts of Europe. Since it takes over 200,000 stigmas to make ½kg of saffron, and each one is hand picked, it is not surprising that this is the world's most expensive spice. It is used to impart subtle flavour and yellow colour, available in stigma or powdered form, it should be used very sparingly. Steep saffron in a little warm water before use. Saffron can be used in rice, meat and poultry dishes, soups and some traditional breads and cakes.

TUMERIC Tumeric is the root of a plant of the ginger family. It is native to India and other parts of Asia. The dried, aromatic root is ground to a deep yellow in colour, it is often a curry ingredient and is used commercially in mustard, curry powder and some pickles. At home, use it in sauces and dressings, marinades for chicken and shellfish and in some pickles and chutneys.

SPICE COMBINATIONS

CURRY POWDER Curry powder is a combination of spices, depending on the country of origin. Flavours vary from mild to very hot. Some ingredients of curry powder may be cumin, coriander, fenugreek, tumeric, ginger, pepper, mace, cardamom, cloves and dried chilli peppers.

MIXED SPICE Mixed spice, as the name implies is a blend of certain spices in finely ground form. Generally there will be caraway, allspice, coriander, cumin, nutmeg and ginger, but other spices, such as cinnamon, may be included. Mixed spice is used in cakes, puddings, and with fruit.

PICKLING SPICES The ingredients included in pickling spices vary in different recipes. It usually includes black peppercorns, red chillies and some of the following spices; mustard seed, allspice, cloves, ginger, mace and coriander seed.

AROMATIC SEEDS

ANISEED Anise is an annual plant growing to ½m in height and producing flat topped bunches of white flowers. The seeds and fresh leaves are used in cooking and its sharp, distinctive aroma is unmistakable in the liqueur Anisette. It is grown mainly for the seeds, although the leaves may be sprinkled over salads. Aniseed flavours shellfish, meat, stuffings, scones, rolls, bread and biscuits.

CARAWAY SEED Caraway is the aromatic seed of a biennial member of the parsley family. It is grown mainly for its seeds, but the roots are also edible; they can be boiled and eaten like carrots. Caraway seed is used to flavour stews, breads, cheeses, soups, vegetables, pickles, meat and fish dishes. Traditionally used in seed cake.

CARDAMOM SEED Cardamom seed is an Indian native plant used extensively in Indian cookery. Cardamom pods, the whole or ground seeds can be bought. The off-white pods are about 1.25cm in length and contain about 12 or 16 seeds. The seeds are very hard, so they should be crushed before use to release their pungent flavour. Whole cardamom seeds are used in fruit punches, pickles, and marinades. In their ground form they are included in bread and cakes, meat balls and roast pork. It is a component of curry powder.

CELERY SEED Celery seed is small and brownish, and has a potent taste. It is the dried fruit of the celery plant. It may be used in seafood cocktails, pickles, chutneys, soups, stews, fish dishes and some vegetable dishes. Commercial celery salt is flavoured with ground celery seed, or with ground dried celery stems.

CORIANDER SEED Coriander is available in whole seed or ground form. The seeds are small, slightly oval, and bleached. It cooks with a comparatively mild spice flavour similar to nutmeg. The longer the seeds are kept (they should be stored in a dry place) the more pronounced the flavour becomes. Seeds can be left whole in cooking but it is usual to crush them first. They are used in both curry powder and pot pourri and give a spicy flavour when added to casseroles and soups.

CUMIN SEED Cumin, a low-growing annual from the Mediterranean, is used in Near and Middle Eastern cookery, and is a basic ingredient of curry powder. The dried ripe fruit of the plant forms the spice and it has a pungent aroma. It is available ground or in whole seed form. Use cumin in pickles, chutneys, rice, pork and lamb dishes.

DILL SEED Dill is an annual plant, a native of southern Europe. It is similar in appearance to fennel, and is grown for its fern-like leaves and for the aromatic buff-coloured seeds which give food added flavour. Either chopped, fresh leaves or seeds can be used. In dill pickles the herb helps to make the cucumber more digestible.

FENNEL SEED Perennial fennel (sweet fennel) and annual Florence fennel are the best two known varieties. Seeds of both can be used in cooking, but leaves and stems of Florence fennel have a more pleasant flavour than those of the perennial; leaves, stems, roots and seed all have an aniseed taste. The raw stems can be cut into 2.5cm (1in) slices and stuffed with cream cheese or used in a salad. The seeds may be cooked with fish or added to bread and pastries. Chop the fresh leaves and add to soups and sauces.

JUNIPER BERRIES Juniper berries are the dried, ripe fruit of a small, evergreen shrub native to Europe, North Africa and Arctic regions. Berries are not mature until the second or third year, when they are picked and dried. New cones form on the tree while the previous berries are ripening from green to silvery purple. Best known as the flavouring in gin, the berries are used in stuffings and marinades for poultry and game and can be added to coleslaw and sauerkraut. Due to their pungency, they should be used sparingly – 4-8 berries, crushed, will generally be sufficient to give the desired piquant flavour.

MUSTARD SEED   The hardy annual mustard plant will grow in almost any temperate area of the world. There are two main varieties, both native to Europe and producing seeds that vary in strength and flavour. Mustard greens can be used in salads, the larger leaves are quite hot. Commercial powdered ginger is a combination of light yellow and dark red seeds of different species, sometimes blended with tumeric. Use mustard seeds sparingly until you become used to them.

POPPY SEED   Poppy seeds are the non-narcotic seeds of the poppy. The seeds may be used whole or ground; the small grains are a natural source of minerals. Valuable oil is extracted from the seed. Sprinkle whole on breads, pastries, salads, pasta, baked or grilled fish. Use ground in cakes or strudel fillings.

SESAME SEED   Sesame is an annual that grows about 1 metre high and has white flowers that are followed by small, flat, light brown, round seeds. The seeds are high in mineral and protein content. In many parts of the world, oil extracted from the seeds is used for cooking. The faintly nutty flavour of the seeds is brought out by 20 minutes in a moderate oven. Sesame seeds are sprinkled on breads, buns, cakes and pastries. They can also be added to cheese mixtures and fish dishes, sprinkled on canapes, added to salad dressings.

VANILLA POD   The vanilla bean is the seed pod of a yellow-flowered orchid native to Central America; the pods are odourless and flavourless. Over a period of 6 months, they are subjected to alternate heat and darkness to induce fermentation. When almost black in colour, the vanilla bean as we know it, emerges, Vanilla extract is produced by steeping the cured pods in a mixtue of alcohol and water.

Keep a vanilla bean in a jar containing sugar – the flavour is imparted to the sugar to be used in cakes and custards. Heat the whole pod, or a small piece, in milk for any sweet dish requiring these two ingredients. The bean can be washed and dried afterwards to be stored and used again. An alternative method is to split the bean and remove the seeds. Store the bean in a sugar jar and used the seeds – the part with the strongest flavour – for heating with milk. Vanilla flavour is popular for many sweet recipes, including custards, ice cream, cakes, puddings and confectionery.

COOKERY TERMS

ACIDIFY To add lemon juice, wine or vinegar to water, a sauce or cooked fish.

AL DENTE An Italian cookery term most often used to describe the cooking of pasta. It means that the spaghetti, noodles, macaroni etc should be cooked until barely tender. (It should retain a bite.)

APERITIF Designed to sharpen the appetite. An alcoholic drink taken before meals.

APPETISER Something to soothe and at the same time excite the palate.

AROMA Describes the fragrance of various dishes and wines.

ASPIC A clear brilliant jelly made from meat, fish or poultry and is used for masking cold savoury foods.

AU BLANC Cooked in white sauce.

AU GRATIN A term applied to certain dishes covered with sauce and breadcrumbs, and browned in the oven or under a grill; served in the dish in which they are baked.

AU NATURAL Food cooked plainly and simply or served raw.

BAKE BLIND To part or fully bake a pie shell without its final filling. Baking beans on foil or greaseproof may be used to prevent the centre of the pie shell rising.

BAKING POWDER A mixture of chemicals used for aerating bread, buns or cake mixtures. Use as directed on the container.

BALMAIN BUG An edible crustacean approximately

15cm (6in) in length (shovel nosed lobster) referred to as Moreton Bay Bugs by Queenslanders. The flesh is similar in flavour to large varieties of lobster and is found in the tail. Bug meat can be served either hot or cold.

BARDING Is using bacon or pork fat to cover the outside of poulty or game, to give a continuous basting in the absence of natural fat.

BASTE To pour or spoon liquid over food as it cooks in order to moisten and flavour.

BATTER A mixture of flour and some liquid, mixed together, it may be thin enough to coat food, pour or be dropped from a spoon.

BEAN SPROUTS Being high in nutrition, bean sprouts are grown from seed to a length of 25-30mm (1-1¼in).

BEATING A brisk whipping action, to introduce air into a mixture to make it smooth and light.

BIND to moisten a mixture with egg, cream or sauce to hold it together.

BESAN FLOUR A staple ingredient in Indian cooking, split peas are gound to form a flour.

BISQUE A rich thick shell fish soup.

BLANCH To put into boiling water, remove, plunge into cold water. Object – to remove strong flavour (onions), to whiten (brains), to cleanse (nuts).

BLEND To combine two or more ingredients together or to chop or puree in a blender or food processor.

BOMBAY DUCK Cured raw fish with strong odour. It becomes appetising when cooked in fat or baked in the oven. Served with curries or crumbled over rice.

BONE To remove the bones from raw or cooked fish, chicken, poultry, game or meat.

BOUILLABAISSE A fish soup made from a mixture of small fish with lobsters, crayfish, saffron, garlic, olive oil, tomato, wine and seasonings.

BOUQUET GARNI A bunch or 'faggot' or herbs, used to flavour stews, casseroles and sauces. Usually consists of fresh sprigs of parsley, thyme, marjoram, rosemary, a bay leaf, peppercorns and cloves, tied in muslin. (If unavailable use dried).

BREADCRUMBS There are three types:–
1 dried – scraps of white bread baked in the oven until dry or light brown and dry, then crushed until fine.
2 buttered or fried – white bread fried in oil or butter until crisp.
3 fresh – stale white bread prepared either by grating or sieving.

BRINE A simple salt water mixture used for preservation, pickling and colour retention of certain fruits (pears, apples).

BROWN TO This is preliminary preparation to the cooking of many stews and casseroles dishes. The meat can be either fried or grilled. This seals in the juices so that the substance of the meat retain more flavour, which browning improves. Also, it gives a better colour.

BUFFET A culinary term referring to a long table on

which food is served.

CANAPE Bite sized pieces of food spread on edible bases, usually bread, then garnished. Served with cocktails.

CARAMELISE To melt sugar in a heavy saucepan until it is a light golden brown syrup.

CAVIAR Prepared from roe from various members of the fish family, including sturgeon, beluga and steret.

CHAPATIS Very large Indian pancakes made with wholemeal flour and water. Cooked in an ungreased frying pan, lightly buttered, fried to a light brown and eaten with curry.

CHEERIOS A small (2½cm, 1in) cocktail frankfurt (Weiner) made from pork or beef, they can be boiled, barbecued or served in a sauce. A little relative to the hot dog.

CHILL To place in refrigerator or other cold place until cold.

CHOP To cut meat, vegetables or fruit, with a quick firm movement into small pieces.

CHOWDER A thick soup made from a variety of food stuffs and often with a milk base. The name chowder is a corruption of the French Chaudiere, a large, heavy pot used by the farmers and fishermen to cook the local soups and stews.

CLARIFY To clear or free fat and liquids from impurities.

COATING To cover fish, cutlets, rissoles etc with:–

1 seasoned flour
2 flour and egg
3 batter
4 egg and breadcrumbs

COMPOTE Fruit cooked in syrup while retaining its shape.

CONCASSEE To remove skin and seeds from tomato, then chop flesh roughly.

CONDIMENTS Seasonings to serve with hot or cold dishes, eg. salt, pepper, mustard, vinegar.

CONSOMME A clear soup.

CREAMING To mix and beat one or more foods (such as butter and sugar) until soft and fluffy.

CREPES French name given to thin pancakes.

CROUTE A thick slice of bread, either fried or toasted.

CROUTONS Thin slices of bread diced into small pieces or fancy shapes and fried. Used for garnishing soups etc.

CRUMB To coat ingredients, previously dipped in seasoned flour, egg or milk or other adhesive mixtures in breadcrumbs.

CRUSTACEAN Crustaces – seafood with a hard shell and jointed extremities, generally aquatic. Some species used in cooking are crabs, crayfish, lobsters etc.

DEHYDRATION A process of removing the water content with food stuffs.

DEVEIN Devein is a process applied to prawns after

the shell has been removed, by making a shallow slit down the back of the prawn and removing the feeding tract.

DHAL Widely used in Indian cooking, notably in soups, curries and savoury dishes, Dhal is basically a variety of dried beans, peas and lentils.

DICE Food cut into small even cubes or pieces.

DILUTING To reduce in strength by adding water or other liquids.

DISJOINT To cut into pieces at the joint.

DISSOLVE To mix a dry ingredient with a liquid until it is dispersed.

DOUBLE BOILER Two saucepans, one fitting snugly on top of the other, in which water in the lower saucepan is kept at simmering or boiling point, or almost at boiling point, so foods are cooked in the top half without direct heat.

DRAIN To remove liquid or fat from foods, by means of a sieve, colander or by placing fried foods on absorbent paper.

DREDGE to coat food with a fine ingredient by dusting, sprinkling or rolling the food in flour, cornflour, sugar, icing sugar.

DRESSED VEGETABLES Vegetables to which additional ingredients have been added to enhance colour contrast, flavour and texture. More elaborate dressed vegetables may be served as a separate course eg petit pois a la Francaise.

DRESSING Liquids used to moisten salad, eg French.

DRIPPING Clarified fat. this is the fat which has been separated from the meat during cooking.

DUCHESSE Potatoes finely mashed with butter, egg yolk and piped through a forcing bag in whirl shapes, then lightly browned in the oven. NB. cream may be added if required.

DUST To sprinkle lightly as with flour or sugar.

EGG WASH A mixture of egg and a little water or milk, used to glaze pastry and bread.

EMULSION A suspension of oil and water, or milk and margarine or butter, beaten together until thoroughly blended to a cream.

ENTREES Dishes served between fish and the main course at dinner.

ENTREMETS Hot or cold desserts, pastries, cakes, ice creams and sorbets.

ESCALOPE A thin slice of meat, fish or poultry usually cut from the fillet. Escalope can refer to almost any thinly sliced food.

EXTRACTS These are obtained from many food stuffs by varying processes, eg meat and yeast extracts.

FAGGOT A small bundle of herbs or vegetables tied together.

FERMENTATION A chemical reaction which produces changes in the characteristics of food stuffs, by the action of bacteria, eg wine making, yeast cookery, cheese making.

FILLET
1 Special cut of beef, lamb, pork or veal, breast of

poultry and game, fish cut off the bone without skin.

2 To cut any of the above to use in cooking.

FLAKE   Pull apart with fork into shreds, eg fish.

FLAKES   Dehydrated vegetable pieces, eg onion.

FLAMBE   to flame foods with a spirit, eg brandy or other fortified wines. The spirit is heated, set alight and poured flaming over the food.

FLAN   An open sweet or savoury tart. Usually made in a special tin from which the rim can be removed.

FLOWERETTES   A term which refers to cauliflower or broccoli when the individual heads have been separated from the stalks.

FOIS GRAS   A paste of fat goose liver.

FOLDING   A method lightly combining beaten egg whites or whipped cream with another mixture so that the air cells are not broken down. Literally folding in the egg whites or cream with a fine edged utensil in a downward cutting motion rather than stirring.

FORCEMEAT   Finely minced ingredients and seasoning used for stuffing birds, meat or vegetables.

GARNISH   They are sometimes named after the place of origin, the person who invented them, or perhaps a special occasion. The object of a garnish is to add colour, flavour, interest and texture to foods. A garnish may be an integral part of a dish, or simply a sprig of watercress.

GATEAU   A rich cake, usually a butter sponge base, richly decorated with cream or butter cream, etc.

GELATINE   A transparent substance derived from beef bones, cartilage and tendons. Usually purchased in a dehydrated form, used as a setting substance.

GEM IRON   A cast iron baking tin similar to muffin or patty tins, used for making gem scones.

GHEE   A clarified butter, originally obtained from the Indian buffalo.

GLAZE   To make food shiny. Aids browning or appearance with egg, water, sugar, etc.

GLUTEN   When the protein of wheat flour is combined with moisture and handled, a substance called gluten is produced. It is an elastic substance which expands when aerated with gases, and it sets when heated.

GOLDEN SYRUP   A light coloured treacle produced by the evaporation of sugar cane juice in the manufacture of crystalline sugar. Used to sweeten, flavour and colour cakes, puddings etc.

GRATE   To reduce to small pieces or granules by using either grater or food processor.

GRAVY   The name given to pan juice liquid thickened with flour.

GREASE   To rub lightly with butter, margarine, oil or fat, to prevent food from sticking.

GRILL (BROIL)   To cook under fierce dry heat from a griller (Broiler) or barbecue.

HORS D'OEUVRE   Finger foods, hot or cold. Served

before a meal, or before the main part of a meal.

HULL To remove or strip the outer covering, in particular from corn.

ICES A water or cream mixture, frozen quickly to produce fine ice particles.

INFUSE To steep in hot liquid without boiling, to extract flavour.

JELLY Obtained by:-
1 boiling of meat and bones
2 cooking fruit, rich in protein
3 sweets made from commercial aids, eg. gelatine.

JULIENNE A garnish of vegetables and meat, cut in match like strips and served with various dishes.

KEBABS Small pieces of meat and vegetables, threaded on a long thin skewer, grilled or barbecued.

KIWI FRUIT Chinese gooseberries, an oval shaped fruit with green flesh and tiny black seeds, the outer skin is a furry fawn colour. The ripe fruit should be soft and served at room temperature.

KNEAD To work dough until it is of the desired consistency or elasticity.

KNOCK BACK A term used in yeast cookery when the dough is first kneaded after proving.

LARD The white fat from the inside of a pig, melted and clarified.

LARDING To thread narrow strips of bacon fat through the surface of uncooked meats.

LEAVENING AGENTS These are raising agents used to make cakes, breads and pastries rise, eg yeast, baking powder, bicarbonate of soda, air.

LEGUME the fruit or edible part of a leguminous plant, eg beans, peas or pulses.

LENTIL Lentils and pulses are seeds of leguminous plants. They are native to Central Asia, where they have been cultivated since prehistoric times. There are numerous varieties. This vegetable contains more protein than any other.

LIAISON A thickening agent designed to give body and gloss to a liquid food, sauce, stock or soup eg. egg yolk, cream or butter.

LOLO Coconut cream which is prepared by addition of water to grated coconut, then squeezed and strained.

MACERATE To soak fruit in flavoured juices, syrups and liquor to impart flavour.

MARASCHINO A sweet liqueur with a highly concentrated flavour distilled from fermented maraschino cherries, usesd to flavour sweet dishes.

MARINATE To stand food in a liquid combination to impart flavour or tenderise.

MASKING To evenly cover or coat food with a sauce, jelly or mayonnaise.

MELT to liquify by heat.

MERINGUE Essentially a mixture of egg whites and sugar stiffly beaten.

MINCE To reduce to very small pieces with a mincer, chopper or knife.

MITI SAUCE Freshly grated coconut is added to chillies, onions, and lemon juice: the residue is then squeezed out.

MIX To combine ingredients in a circular motion in a bowl or saucepan.

MOCHA A combination of coffee and chocolate flavours.

MOUSSE A light, aerated mixtue of eggs, cream and gelatine which can be savoury (meat, poultry, game or fish) or sweet (fruit puree, chocolate etc). Mostly served cold or even iced, though a few can be eaten hot.

NOISETTES
1 meat cut from loin fillet of either lamb, veal, pork or beef
2 a dish made with hazelnuts
3 potatoes scooped out in the shape of hazelnuts and browned in butter.

OFFAL OR VARIETY MEAT An animal's offal consists of the skin, feet, tail, horns, head and tongue, the lung, liver, spleen and pancreas known as the pluck, the intestines and any other edible internal organ.

PARBOIL To boil until partially cooked.

PARE OR PEEL To remove outside skin or covering of fruits or vegetables with a knife or vegetable peeler, eg orange or potato.

PATE A mixture of finely ground meats, liver or game, seasoned and flavoured.

PAVLOVA A soft centred meringue dessert made from egg white and sugar. Pavlova is traditionally accompanied by whipped cream, fresh strawberries and passionfruit. Pavlova was created in a Perth hotel in 1935 in honour of the Russian Ballerina Anna Pavlova.

PASTA An Italian word for products made from flour egg and liquid and shaped eg spaghetti, macaroni.

PASTEURIZE A heat treatment of food to kill harmful micro-organisms without imparing the quality.

PAW PAW A tropical yellow melon type fruit originally from Central America correctly referred to as *papaya*. It is used in salads, ice cream, drinks, chutneys. Paw Paw is so versatile it can be used with sweet and savoury foods.

PESTLE & MORTAR A piece of kitchen equipment used for pounding ingredients to make them smooth or into a paste. The mortar is a thick bowl of marble or wood, stone or metal, and the pestle usually of wood or wood and stone combined.

PETIT FOURS Bite sized fancy cakes, biscuits or other dainties, usually served with the dessert course.

PHYLO (Fillo) A plain, paper-thin, flour and water pastry used in Greek and middle eastern Turkish sweet and savoury pastries and pies.

PICKLE Vegetables or fruits preserved in well seasoned and spiced vinegar.

PIE A dish of meat, fruit, vegetable or fish covered with a crust and baked.

PILAU (Pilaff) A rice based dish, which can be either a sweet or savoury. The addition of ingredients depends upon the country of origin.

PINCH The amount of powder which can be held between the thumb and fore-finger.

PIPING A method of shaping, cream, potatoes and icings using a pipe and bag.

PIT To remove pit, stone or seed, eg cherries, olives.

POTATO CHIPS Best made from waxy varieties, washed, peeled and cut into 8cm (2½in) matchsticks and deep fried in hot oil.

POUND To reduce to very small pieces, powder or a paste, with a mortar and pestle.

PRAWNS An edible crustacean. Australian varieties include king prawns, tiger prawns, school prawns, Banana prawns and royal red. In America and Asia prawns are commonly referred to as shrimp.

PREHEAT To have oven or cooking appliance at desired temperature before putting food in.

PROFITEROLES Small puffs of choux pastry filled with various savoury and sweet mixtures.

PROVE The filling of yeasted dough with gas as a result of fermentation. A dough has proved when it retains the imprint of a finer that is pressed lightly on the surface.

PUREE To press food through a fine sieve or put in a food blender to produce a smooth thick mixture.

QUICHE A flan or tart with a savoury custard filling.

RAGOUT A stew made from regular size pieces of meat, poultry or fish, sauteed in fat and simmered with stock, meat juices or water or a combination of these, until tender.

RAISING AGENTS Refer to leavening agents.

RANCID Foods of a high fat content in a state of decomposition. They produce a rank taste and smell.

REDUCE To boil a liquid down in order to concentrate flavour and to reduce volume.

REFRESH To stop the cooking process by immediately plunging cooked foods into cold water.

RICE PAPER Made from the edible pith of a Formosan tree, used to wrap sweet and savoury foods.

ROE Eggs and milt of fish. There are two types - hard and soft. The hard roe is the female and the soft is the male.

SAUCE A thickened liquid served with different foods to enhance their flavour and appearance.

SAUTE (Sauter) To cook over a high heat in fat or oil, shaking the pan, and making whatever is in it "sauter" or jump, to keep it from sticking to the bottom.

SCALD To heat to temperature just below boiling point, with small bubbles rising occasionally to the surface.

SCORE To make evenly spaced shallow slits or cuts with a knife, on the surface of food before cooking.

SEAR To brown the surface of meat, fish or poultry, over a fierce heat.

SEASONING This applies to pepper and salt, but also refers to forcemeat and stuffing.

SEGMENT Sections of citrus fruits, free of pith, seed and membrane.

SHERBET Made in the same way as water ices, after freezing, stiffly beaten egg whites are added.

SHORTENING Applies to fats used in making bread, cakes, pastries etc.

SHRED To slice so thinly that pieces curl, or into very fine strips.

SIMMER Occasional bubbles gently breaking on the surface just before boiling.

SKIM To remove foam, fat or solid substance from the surface of a cooking, or cooked mixture.

SLIVER To chop food, especially nuts into thin strips.

SORBET Refer to sherbet.

SOUFFLE Sweet or savoury, made of ingredients cooked to a puree, thickened with yolks of eggs, and with stiffly beaten egg whites folded in, poured into a souffle dish and baked in the oven. The same name has been extended to include quite different preparations, more like mousses or mousselines, served both hot or cold.

SOY SAUCE A sauce used in Asian cooking which is made from fermented soy beans and may be diluted to taste.

STEEP To soak in hot or cold liquid.

STIR To mix in a circular motion with a spoon.

STOCK Is the unseasoned liquid obtained by simmering various substances, eg meat, fish, poultry and vegetables.

SUET The hard dry fat surrounding the kidneys of beef, lamb and pork. Beef suet is the most commonly used variety in Australian cookery. Its dry texture makes it excellent for pastry making particularly for savoury pie crusts and steamed puddings.

SYRUP A solution of sugar and water or fruity juice boiled to a thick consistency.

TOSS To mix lightly, especially salad of fresh greens, using a fork or spoon.

TRUSS To secure poultry and game with skewers and string to keep their shape during cooking.

VINAIGRETTE Basic French dressing of good wine, vinegar, oil, salt, pepper and fresh herbs to taste.

WATER BATH Refer to Bain Marie.

WHIP OR WHISK The process of incorporating air into cream or egg whites until stiff or thick.

ZEST The outside rind of any citrus fruit, which contains the essential oils. It is scraped off the fruit with a fine grater, or by rubbing with a lump of sugar.

NOTES

NOTES

AUSTRALIAN HISTORICAL DATES

1770 British explorer, Captain James Cook, landed at Botany Bay.

1788 First fleet of convicts and free settlers sailed into Sydney Cove and established white settlement.

1797 Captain John Macarthur imported merino sheep – creation of the wool industry.

1798 Bass and Flinders circumnavigated Tasmania.

1804 Tasmania settled.

1813 Blaxland, Lawson and Wentworth crossed the Blue Mountains – pathway to western NSW.

1824 First settlement in Queensland.

1830 South Australia founded.

1835 John Batman founded the city of Melbourne, now the capital of Victoria.

1849 Deportation of convicts from Britain ended throughout Australia.

1850 Victoria established as a separate colony.

1851 Beginning of the gold rush in NSW and Victoria.

1852 University of Sydney founded.

1854 Eureka Stockade at Ballarat, Victoria.

1859 Queensland founded.

1872 Overland telegraph opened.

1883 Bushranger Ned Kelly hung.

1883 Minerals discovered in the Silver City, Broken Hill.

1900 Australian Commonwealth established.

1901 Federation of all Australian states.

1915 Australia and New Zealand Army Corps (ANZACS) landed at Gallipoli, Turkey – First World War.

1927 Opening of Parliament House, Canberra, ACT.

1932 Sydney Harbour Bridge opened.

1942 Darwin, N.T. bombed by Japanese.

1949 Commencement of Snowy Mountains hydro-electric scheme.

1956 Olympic Games held in Melbourne, Victoria.

1956 Television in Australia.

1966 Decimal currency.

1974 Sydney Opera House opened by Queen Elizabeth II.

1974 Cyclone Tracy, Darwin N.T.

1976 Granville, NSW train disaster.

1977 Centenary Cricket Test between Australia and England.

1980 Dingo suspected of taking Azaria Chamberlain at Ayers Rock, N.T.

1982 Commonwealth Games Brisbane, Qld.

1983 Australia wins America's Cup.

1984 The Little Aussie Cookbook launched.

1988 Australia's Bicentenary.

North

Prawns

DARWIN

Oysters
Kingcrabs

Beef

Beef
Dates
Figs

Barramundi

Coral Trout

Mangoes
Paw Paw
Sugar Cane
Ginger
Rum
Bananas
Peanuts
Pineapple

Beef

AUSTRALIA

BRISBANE

Lamb

Fruit

Dairy Products

Oysters
Rock Lobsters
Prawns

PERTH

Avocadoes
Wheat

Lamb

Wheat
Wine
Grapes

Wheat
Lamb

Dairy Products
Rock Oysters

Crayfish

Lobsters

ADELAIDE

Citrus Fruit
Stone Fruit
Wine

SYDNEY

CANBERRA

Tuna

MELBOURNE

Flounder

Apples
Tasmanian Scallops

Potatoes

HOBART

Advance Australia Fair

Australians all let us rejoice,
For we are young and free;
We've golden soil and wealth for toil,
Our home is girt by sea.
Our land abounds in nature's gifts
Of beauty rich and rare;
In history's page, let every stage
Advance Australia fair.
In joyful strains then let us sing,
Advance Australia fair.

Beneath our radiant Southern Cross
We'll toil with hearts and hands,
To make this Commonwealth of ours
Renowned of all the lands.
For those who've come across the seas
We've boundless plans to share,
With courage let us all combine
To Advance Australia fair.
In joyful strains then let us sing,
Advance Australia fair.

NATIONAL ANTHEM

MICHELLE MIRAN

Born in Waverley, a near seaside suburb of Sydney, New South Wales, Michelle is a second generation Australian of Polish/Jewish background. She first trained as a home economist at East Sydney Technical College, Darlinghurst.

A Bachelor of Education graduate from the Sydney College of Advanced Education, she has taught home economics specialising in the history and geography of food for over a decade in high schools and technical colleges. Michelle is currently Head of Division, Special Courses, School of Home Science in Technical and Further Education – a statewide responsibility.

Over the years, Michelle has extensively travelled through Europe and Asia, broadening her interest in wines and foods of all nations and their culinary history. She entertains extensively at home, often experimenting with new and creative recipes – a true gourmet! Michelle has a strong commitment in pursuing the development of multicultralism in Australia.

GEORGE JAKSIC

Born in Paddington, of Serbian (Yugoslav) parents, George, who is bilingual, was educated at Fort Street Boys' High School. He completed a Bachelor of Arts degree majoring in geography and government at the University of Sydney.

In 1974, using technical skills obtained during his studies and refined while editing a university student magazine, he commenced an artwork and graphic design service. Since then, the Honeysett Printing Group of companies have been incorporated and, as managing director, he heads a diverse, independent printing operation that uses sophisticated computerised equipment and provides consultancy, art studio facilities and trade services. The establishment of Honeysett Publications has enabled the development of a variety of projects such as "The Little Aussie Cookbook".

A keen gourmet (he'll try anything once!) who has travelled around Europe, Asia and the Pacific, George dines regularly with friends at exotic eateries which are often the source of his culinary inspiration.

INDEX

✂ ORDER COUPON

THE LITTLE AUSSIE COOKBOOK
Honeysett Publications Pty Ltd
PO Box 23, Westgate NSW 2048 Australia

Please rush me   copy/ies of THE LITTLE AUSSIE COOKBOOK, at *$A8.00 each (post and handling included within Australasia, elsewhere overseas add extra $A2.00 per book). Enclosed is my cheque / M.O. for $ payable to Honeysett Publications
OR debit my Visa or Bankcard for $A ....

NO. ☐☐☐☐☐☐☐☐☐☐☐☐☐☐☐☐ Visa/Bankcard *(circle one)*

Expiry Date .... Signature ....

NAME ....

ADDRESS ....

.... P'CODE .... STATE ....

✂ ORDER COUPON

THE LITTLE AUSSIE COOKBOOK
Honeysett Publications Pty Ltd
PO Box 23, Westgate NSW 2048 Australia

Please rush me   copy/ies of THE LITTLE AUSSIE COOKBOOK, at *$A8.00 each (post and handling included within Australasia, elsewhere overseas add extra $A2.00 per book). Enclosed is my cheque / M.O. for $ payable to Honeysett Publications
OR debit my Visa or Bankcard for $A ....

NO. ☐☐☐☐☐☐☐☐☐☐☐☐☐☐☐☐ Visa/Bankcard *(circle one)*

Expiry Date .... Signature ....

NAME ....

ADDRESS ....

.... P'CODE .... STATE ....